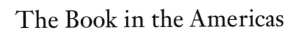

The Book in the Americas

Sponsored by

THE LAMPADIA FOUNDATION

THE NATIONAL ENDOWMENT FOR THE HUMANITIES

FOMENTO EDUCACIONAL, A.C. (MEXICO)

THE FRANK M. BARNARD FOUNDATION

The Book in the Americas

THE ROLE OF BOOKS AND PRINTING IN THE DEVELOPMENT OF CULTURE AND SOCIETY IN COLONIAL LATIN AMERICA

CATALOGUE OF AN EXHIBITION BY

Julie Greer Johnson

WITH A BIBLIOGRAPHICAL SUPPLEMENT

BY SUSAN L. NEWBURY

PROVIDENCE · RHODE ISLAND

THE JOHN CARTER BROWN LIBRARY

MCM · LXXXVIII

THE JOHN CARTER BROWN LIBRARY IS AN
INDEPENDENTLY FUNDED AND ADMINISTERED CENTER FOR ADVANCED
RESEARCH IN THE HUMANITIES AT BROWN UNIVERSITY

COPYRIGHT © 1988 BY THE JOHN CARTER BROWN LIBRARY

ISBN 0–916617–30–0

PRINTED IN THE UNITED STATES OF AMERICA BY
MERIDEN-STINEHOUR PRESS, LUNENBURG, VERMONT
AND MERIDEN, CONNECTICUT

CONTENTS

ILLUSTRATIONS

FOREWORD

"I‍T IS HARD to imagine an activity involving so many aspects of national life as does book publishing," Laurence Hallewell observes in his ground-breaking work, *Books in Brazil* (1982). "The book exists to give literary expression to cultural and ideological values. Its design is the interface of aesthetics and the available technology. Its manufacture requires the supply of particular industrial products (which may be imported, made from imported raw materials, or wholly manufactured locally). Its marketing is a commercial process conditioned by geographic, economic, educational, social, and political factors. And the whole provides an excellent measure of a country's degree of dependence or independence, both spiritual and material."

The history of books is endlessly fascinating, in other words, because few other products of human society are so reflective of the world around them or of the world from which they spring. Books are part of a complex and organic cultural system, and their history cannot be studied without reference also to modes of education; literacy and the psychology of reading; authorship as a vocation; the technology of book production; the establishment of agencies for publishing and distributing books; the impact or influence of books and reading on society, politics, and culture; and the interrelationship of the production and distribution of books with such institutions as the nation-state and the church.

It has been five hundred years since Gutenberg produced the first printed book as we know it, and for most of that time the book has been the pre-eminent concrete medium of communication, the indispensable mode of information storage and of documentation both sacred and profane, the principal means by which illustration has been broadcast, the supreme outlet for the literary imagination, a major source of entertainment, and the basis of most formal instruction, to mention only those dimensions of the book that seem most salient.

In the twentieth century, however, with the invention of new media that can substitute for the printed book in numerous ways—one thinks, obviously, of films and photographs, television and photocopiers, slick magazines and the now nearly ubiquitous computer—it is clear that the unique "era of the book" has drawn to a close. Such profound changes in our cultural life stimulate fresh historical investigation, for we now find ourselves able to view the past of the book with a detachment that fifty years ago would have been impossible to achieve. With that detachment has come a spate of historical monographs and conferences on the role and impact of the printed book in the development of Western society and culture.

L'histoire du livre as a field of interdisciplinary study has burgeoned in the past twenty-five years in France, England, Germany, and the United States. Relatively less attention, however, has been given in this period to the history of books and printing in Spain, Portugal, and Latin America, despite distinguished beginnings in the work of such scholars as the prodigious José Toribio Medina and Irving Leonard, to mention just two names.

In the case of colonial Latin America, the interrelationships of the history of the book with the institutions of church and state are particularly complex, with the Catholic Church desiring to promote education but also to limit the circulation of books through such institutions as the Inquisition. However that may be, printing was introduced into Mexico less than fifty years after the discovery of the Western Hemisphere (and only eighty or ninety years after printing with movable metal type began in Europe), and it has been estimated that during the colonial period some 17,000 titles were published in Spanish America. The history of book printing in the Western Hemisphere becomes all the more interesting when examined in comparative perspective. For example, in contrast to Spanish America, where the printing of books began in Mexico less than twenty-five years after the conquest, or British America, where books also began to be printed in Massachusetts within twenty-five years of English settlement in the region, almost no printing or publishing was permitted or developed in Brazil before the nineteenth century.

At the John Carter Brown Library there has been a long and continuous tradition of interest in the history of the book. Few other libraries in the world, if any, have a larger collection of books printed in the Americas as a whole before 1800. George Parker Winship in 1912, when he was the Librarian of the John Carter Brown, discovered and identified the first work to appear from a press in South America, *Pragmática sobre los diez días del año*, and among the many contributions to the history of the book by Lawrence C. Wroth, Librarian from 1924 to 1957, were *The Colonial Printer* (1931) and *An American Bookshelf, 1755* (1934).

The origins of the present exhibition catalogue are inseparable from a larger, related undertaking of the Library of which this catalogue is a part. With the new interdisciplinary interest in the history of the book, it seemed almost obligatory that the JCB make a contribution of its own to the subject. All that was needed was the right conjunction of people. In the summer of 1984, Julie Greer Johnson, a professor at the University of Georgia specializing in colonial Latin American literature, was invited to the Library as a Research Fellow for three months. Her project was "Satire in Colonial Spanish American Literature," a subject on which she was writing a monograph. In the course of her stay at the Library discussions ensued on the history of the book as an artifact in colonial Latin America, with the happy outcome that Professor Johnson agreed to work with the staff of the John Carter Brown Library in the organization of an international scholarly conference on the subject and on the preparation of a special exhibition and exhibition catalogue.

By the early spring of 1985 Professor Johnson had written a prospectus for the conference, which included a full statement of the rationale for it and a review of earlier work. "A conference on the 'Book in the Americas' with primary emphasis on colonial

Latin America would be a significant contribution to the universal history of the book for two main reasons," Professor Johnson wrote. "First, a review of past studies undertaken in the area reveals their limited perspective and their incompleteness, and second, a glance at the research possibilities underscores the uniqueness of the book's development in the New World." The conference, we hoped, would (1) provide a survey of available sources and past bibliographical information, (2) identify inadequacies in existing scholarship, and (3) open up new areas of research and stimulate interest in their investigation.

The organization of the scholarly conference was fully elaborated in the summer of 1985 at a meeting of a planning committee assembled for this purpose. The members of the planning committee were: Sara Castro-Klarén, at the time Chief of the Hispanic Division of the Library of Congress; David D. Hall, Professor of History at Boston University and Chairman, Program in the History of the Book in American Culture at the American Antiquarian Society; Albert Harkness, a retired Foreign Service officer and former Assistant Director of the United States Information Agency; Professor Johnson; Murdo J. MacLeod, Professor of History at the University of Florida; W. Michael Mathes, Professor of History at the University of San Francisco and Honorary Curator of Mexicana at the California State Library, Sutro Branch; John V. Murra, Professor of Anthropology at Cornell University; Antonio Rodríguez-Buckingham, Professor in the School of Library Science at the University of Southern Mississippi; and J. Benedict Warren, Professor of History at the University of Maryland. I wish to express here the gratitude of the Library for the assistance offered by this group. The meeting of the planning committee, which took place in Washington, D.C., was underwritten in part by a small, but timely, grant from the Frank M. Barnard Foundation.

With plans for the conference underway, application was made to the National Endowment for the Humanities for full implementation of the project. It was primarily the award of a grant by the NEH in April of 1986 that made the conference a reality, but the NEH grant was supplemented by support also from Fomento Educacional of Mexico, which enabled six scholars from Mexico to attend the conference, and by a contribution also from José E. Mindlin of São Paulo, Brazil, who made it possible for two scholars from Brazil to be present.

Mr. Mindlin was instrumental as well in introducing the Library's "Book in the Americas" project to the Lampadia Foundation, which not only contributed to the conference but which also underwrote, through a generous grant, the publication of the present exhibition catalogue. It is a pleasure to acknowledge here with gratitude the invaluable assistance of Lampadia and Mr. Paul Hirsch, the Foundation's director, in giving the "Book in the Americas" exhibition permanent embodiment in this catalogue.

The catalogue, and the bibliographical supplement included in it, were both copyedited by Patricia H. Marks of Princeton, New Jersey, who stepped in at a crucial time, when the work was much in need of a firm and experienced hand, and prepared the manuscript for publication. We wish to acknowledge also the courtesy of Professor

W. Michael Mathes, who as honorary curator of the Sutro Collection, arranged for the loan to the John Carter Brown Library of four titles that were included in the exhibition and in this catalogue.

Of course, the "Book in the Americas" conference itself provided enrichment to this catalogue. In this sense, the exhibition, the catalogue, and the conference are all part of a single project. The final element in the project will be the publication of an anthology of the essays presented at the conference, which the Library will bring out in 1989, the 450th anniversary (by the most common reckoning) of the advent of printing in the Western Hemisphere.

NORMAN FIERING
Director & Librarian

PREFACE & ACKNOWLEDGMENTS

ENTRIES in this catalogue are arranged to facilitate a narrative description of the development of printing in the New World and its influence on colonial society. The material is organized according to generally accepted geopolitical divisions of the colonial empires, but these rubrics do not necessarily reflect the names of territories at the time the works were published. Titles of the volumes listed in the catalogue are accurate transcriptions of those appearing on the title pages of the original works. Consequently they reproduce the inconsistencies of colonial orthography and accentuation. The typography and capitalization, however, have been modernized.

Several works were especially helpful as sources for the information in this catalogue: *Annual Reports (1901–1966) of the John Carter Brown Library*, 8 vols. (Providence: The John Carter Brown Library and The Colonial Society of Massachusetts, 1972); Howard Cline, *Guide to the Ethnohistorical Sources, Part Three*, Vol. 14 of the *Handbook of Middle American Indians*, edited by Robert Wauchope (Austin: University of Texas Press, 1975); Laurence Hallewell, *Books in Brazil* (Metuchen, N.J., and London: Scarecrow Press, 1982); Douglas C. McMurtrie, *The First Printing in South America* (Providence: The John Carter Brown Library, 1926); Antonio Rodríguez-Buckingham, "Colonial Peru and the Printing Press of Antonio Ricardo" (Ph.D. diss., University of Michigan, 1977); Hensley C. Woodbridge and Lawrence J. Thompson, *Printing in Colonial Spanish America* (Troy, N.Y.: Whitson Publishing Company, 1976).

I wish to express my gratitude to the staff of the John Carter Brown Library for the expertise and encouragement offered to me in the preparation of the catalogue for the exhibition. The "Bibliographical Supplement" by Susan L. Newbury and the photographs by Richard N. Hurley are invaluable contributions to its presentation. Ilse E. Kramer and Susan Danforth provided vital assistance at various stages of the catalogue's production, and support was also patiently given by Adelina Azevedo, Gunther Buchheim, Lily Capaldi, María Elena Cassiet, Karen De Maria, Lynne A. Harrell, Dennis C. Landis, Franna Low, Leslie T. Olsen, and Elaine Shiner.

Other influential advisors for the project include Professors José Amor y Vázquez and Stephanie Merrim of Brown University, Raquel Chang-Rodríguez of City College of the City University of New York, Enrique Pupo-Walker of Vanderbilt University, Merle E. Simmons of Indiana University, and Wanda Turnley of the Benson Latin American Collection at the University of Texas. Specific suggestions for the catalogue were made by William C. Bryant, Rick Hendricks, Jeffrey H. Kaimowitz, W. Michael Mathes, Lorene Pouncey, Susan Quinlan, Nancy Troike, J. Benedict Warren, and Hensley Woodbridge.

JULIE GREER JOHNSON

Athens, Georgia
January, 1988

ꝗ Uerdadera relacion de la conquista del Peru
y prouincia del Cuzco llamada la nueua Castilla: Conquistada por el magnifico
y esforçado cauallero Francisco piçarro hijo del capitan Gonçalo piçarro caua
llero de la ciudad de Trugillo: como capitan general de la cesarea y catholica
magestad ol emperador y rey nro señor: Embiada a su magestad por Francisco
de Xerez natural de la muy noble y muy leal ciudad de Seuilla secretario del
sobredicho señor en todas las puincias y conquista de la nueua Castilla y vno
de los primeros conquistadores della. ꝗ ꝗ ꝗ ꝗ ꝗ ꝗ ꝗ ꝗ ꝗ ꝗ ꝗ
ꝗ fue vista y examinada esta obra por mandado de los señores inquisidores
del arçobispado de Seuilla: z impressa en casa de Bartholome perez: en el mes
de Julio. Año del parto virginal mil z quinientos y treynta y quatro. ꝗ ꝗ

FRONTISPIECE. FRANCISCO DE XEREZ, *Verdadera relación.* (See p. 52).

INTRODUCTION

As the celebration of the quincentennial of Columbus's landfall approaches in 1992, we are reminded of the common heritage of the Americas and invited to reflect upon the accomplishments of the past that have shaped contemporary society. The history of the book in the former Spanish and Portuguese colonies of the New World, which today constitute countries of Latin America, is an important measure of human progress in the Western Hemisphere. The essential qualities of both the indigenous populations and the conquering nations are embodied in the literary culture of Latin America, and the study of the history of the book therefore provides clear evidence of the high level of their cultural achievements.

Columbus had not yet discovered America when Gutenberg began printing with movable type, but less than a hundred years after its invention, his technology was introduced into the New World by the Spaniards. In 1539, only twenty years after Hernán Cortés's meeting with the Aztec chieftain, Moctezuma, the first book was printed in Tenochtitlán (or Mexico as the Spaniards called it). More amazing, however, is the fact that a form of the book had already existed in Mesoamerica for several centuries. The production of pictorial or ideographic manuscripts did not cease with the fall of Amerindian civilizations but became an early means of communication between friars and their native converts. From the valley of Anáhuac to South America's southern cone, the book accompanied the Spaniards, and they endeavored to establish its production wherever a clear need for it was expressed. By the end of their three-hundred-year domination of the Americas they had developed an entire network of presses throughout the viceroyalties, even in the dense continental jungles.

The history of the book in Brazil adds a dramatic chapter to this extraordinary story of human achievement in the New World. Despite the absence or suppression of the press during the early years of the colonial period, a single event, the Napoleonic invasion of the Iberian peninsula, transformed the history and culture of this Portuguese colony. With the arrival of the French on the outskirts of Lisbon, the royal court was transferred to South America, and with it came the government printing office to meet the needs of an exiled elite.

The exhibition was mounted originally for the conference on "The Book in the Americas" held at the John Carter Brown Library in June, 1987. Its purpose was to document not only the physical aspects of bookmaking but to illustrate as well the book's role in society. In order to reconcile the broad scope of this project with the obvious constraints of space and time, the works on exhibit could only suggest the breadth and depth of the holdings of the John Carter Brown Library. Several extremely rare works were lent by the Sutro Library, and these are identified in the text of the catalogue; we are grateful for the assistance of Professor W. Michael Mathes, honorary curator of Sutro's Mexicana collection.

The earliest examples of New World typography were the focus of the exhibition, and attention was given to the representation of diverse disciplines. Viewed as a whole, therefore, the display suggested the intricate mosaic of colonial Latin American society and culture, touching upon such pertinent topics as the transfer of European technology, the assimilation of the Indian, the growth of institutions of higher learning, the creativity of artists and writers, and the emergence of a national consciousness.

Spanish America

THE BOOK AND PRINTING IN
SPANISH AMERICA

IN MANY RESPECTS, 1492 was a crucial year for Spain. The conquest of the last Moorish kingdom in the Iberian peninsula and the expulsion of the Jews made possible the religious unification of a state that had achieved political solidarity just twenty-three years earlier with the marriage of Isabella of Castile and Ferdinand of Aragon. Columbus's discovery of America, which became known in Europe in March 1493, offered the Spanish crown the ideal opportunity to maintain the exhilarating force it had gathered for the reconquest of the peninsula. The discovery also afforded Europeans a chance to begin again and to create a perfect world through careful planning and supervision. The task of building a new society from its foundations, however, proved to be a formidable undertaking, for the existence of large, sedentary Indian populations required the prudent and lengthy assimilation of American natives into the Spanish way of life.

The Catholic Church was instrumental in realizing the social and political goals of the Spanish crown in the New World. Augustinians, Dominicans, Franciscans, Jesuits, and members of other religious orders participated in the conversion of the Indians to Christianity, and as the earliest European educators, scholars, writers, and book collectors, they laid the groundwork for the continuous and stable growth of Spanish American society. Although their printing presses, institutions of higher learning, and libraries underwent gradual secularization, the Church's influence on colonial life was constant and remained long after political changes had altered the course of the hemisphere's history.

Apart from the clergy's demands for vocabularies, grammars, and doctrinal works, the laity as well required the services of a press. Mexico City and Lima, with their viceregal courts and universities, were cultural and intellectual centers, and works of literature, history, music, and science were produced to meet the needs of an educated elite. The intelligentsia also sought immediate access to information, a desire that prompted the establishment of newspapers. During the independence movement, the efficiency and effectiveness of the periodical press made it an indispensable forum for nationalist expression.

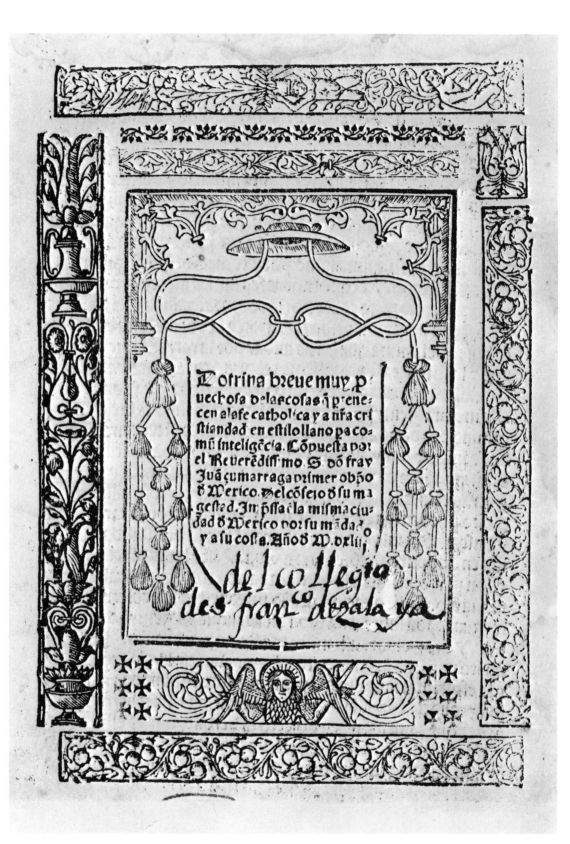

FIG. I. JUAN DE ZUMÁRRAGA, *Dotrina breve* (enlarged).

The Viceroyalty of New Spain

THE AUDIENCIA OF MEXICO

I.

JUAN DE ZUMÁRRAGA (1468–1548). *Dotrina breve muy p[ro]vechosa delas cosas q[ue] p[er]tenecen ala fe catholica y a n[uest]ra cristiandad.* Mexico, [1544].

Juan de Zumárraga, the Franciscan friar who went to Mexico City as its first Bishop in 1528, was instrumental in the introduction of the printing press into the Spanish American colonies. Religious materials were urgently needed for the conversion of the natives, and European printers were ill-equipped to handle manuscripts in Indian languages. At the Bishop's insistence, Juan Cromberger established a branch of his Sevillian publishing house in Mexico City and shipped to the New World all the equipment and supplies vital to its operation. Juan Pablos (d. 1560), a native of Brescia, Italy, became Cromberger's Mexican agent and later the owner of the press on which he printed the 1539 edition of the *Breve y más compendiosa doctrina christiana en lengua mexicana y castellana*, the first American book. Today, the 1544 edition (fig. 1) is the earliest example of a book printed by Pablos's press in American collections.

2.

GABRIEL BIEL (d. 1495). *Repertorium generale & succinctum: veru[m] tame[n] valde utile atq[ue] necessariu[m]: contentoru[m] in quatuor collectoriis, acutissimi ac profundissimi theologi Gabrielis Biel super quatuor libros sententiarum.* Lyon, 1527.
LENT BY THE SUTRO LIBRARY, SAN FRANCISCO.

This treatise on the Gospels belonged to Fray Juan de Zumárraga's personal library, which contained more than four hundred volumes at the time of his death in 1548. The title page (fig. 2) bears his signature. In 1536, the book was presented to the first European academic library in the Americas, established in the Colegio Imperial de Santa Cruz at Santiago Tlatelolco. During his stay in Spain (1532–1534), Zumárraga's petitions to the crown led to the foundation of the Colegio, one of the earliest institutions of learning in the New World.

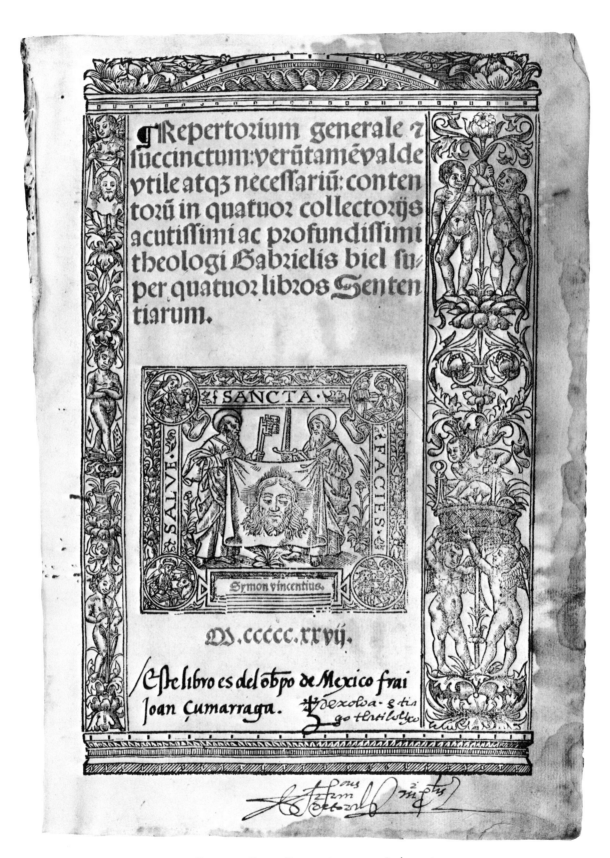

¶Repertorium generale ꝫ
ſuccinctum: verũtamẽ valde
vtile atꝗ neceſſariũ: conten
torũ in quatuor collectorꝗs
acutiſſimi ac profundiſſimi
theologi Gabrielis biel ſu-
per quatuor libros Senten
tiarum.

SANCTA

SALVE FACIES

Symon vincentius.

M.cccc.xxvij.

Eſte libro es del obpo de Mexico frai
Joan Çumarraga.

FIG. 2. GABRIEL BIEL, *Repertorium generale & succinctum.*

3·

MIGUEL DE MEDINA (1489–1578). *De sacrorum hominum continentia libri v.* Venice, 1569.

LENT BY THE SUTRO LIBRARY, SAN FRANCISCO.

FIG. 3. MIGUEL DE MEDINA, *De sacrorum hominum continentia.*

As an important educational center in New Spain, the Colegio Imperial de Santa Cruz at Santiago Tlatelolco attracted numerous scholars, who consulted the many volumes of its extensive library. This theological work (fig. 3), once in the Colegio's library, bears the signature of the Franciscan missionary Fray Juan Baptista and was designated for his *use* only (*ad usum*). Because he was a member of a mendicant order, he was not permitted to own any personal property.

Fray Juan Baptista, who was born in New Spain, entered the Franciscan Order at the great convent of Mexico and taught philosophy there. He spent his later years at Tlatelolco, where he served as guardian and became one of the leading authorities on the Nahuatl language. Between 1599 and 1601, his well-known *Confessionario en lengua mexicana y castellana* and several other bilingual works were printed at the Colegio by Melchor Ocharte.

4·

JEAN GERSON (1363–1429). *Tripartito del christianissimo y consolatorio doctor Juan Gerson de doctrina christiana.* Mexico, 1544.

The Inquisition, established in Lima in 1570 and in Mexico City in 1571, became the principal agency judging the acceptability of manuscripts and books, serving also as a court to hear cases when laws were broken. Before then, censorship of the press in colonial Spanish America was the responsibility of both civil and ecclesiastical authorities. Permission to publish was obtained from the Church's highest ranking official in the viceroyalty. As stated on the title page of the *Tripartito*, the volume was reviewed and approved by order of Bishop Zumárraga (fig. 4). The publishing house is given

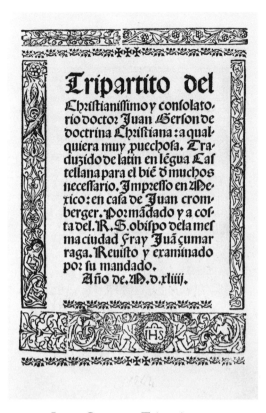

FIG. 4. JEAN GERSON, *Tripartito*.

here as the "Casa de Juan Cromberger," a custom that would be maintained in the printing of the colophon until 1548.

This translation of Gerson's work, which had first appeared in Latin in 1467, is another example of Juan Pablos's printing. The book is notable because it contains the first full-page book illustration, following a European format, printed in the New World. Because of the scarcity of such woodcuts, this one was used again by other early Mexican printers. The verso of the title page depicts a scene in which Saint Ildefonso receives the chasuble from the Virgin Mary (fig. 5).

5.

NEW SPAIN. *Ordena[n]ças y copilacion de leyes: hechas por el muy illustre señor don Antonio d[e] Me[n]doça Visorey y Governador desta Nueva España: y Preside[n]te de la Audie[n]cia Real q[ue] en ella reside: y por los Señores Oydores d[e] la dicha audie[n]cia: p[ar]a la bue[n]a governacio[n] y estilo d[e] los oficiales della.* Mexico, 1548.

In addition to producing religious materials, Juan Pablos also published a number of secular works. Among them was the *Ordenanças*, the first law book printed in the New World. It was compiled by the first Viceroy of New Spain, Antonio de Mendoza, who served in that post from 1535 to 1550. In the latter year he was appointed Viceroy of Peru, where he served until his death in 1552.

This sixteenth title issued by the first American press is an extraordinary example of early Gothic-letter typography (fig. 6). Only two copies are known to exist: this one from the Sutro Library which was originally a part of the library at the Franciscan monastery of Texcoco, and the one in the Lenox Collection of the New York Public Library. The laws included in the *Ordenanças* were later incorporated into the better-

Aue Maria gratia

plena dominus tecū.

FIG. 5. Saint Ildefonso and the Virgin, from JEAN GERSON, *Tripartito* (enlarged).

known *Philippys Hispaniarum et Indiarum Rex*, compiled by Doctor Vasco de Puga (who served as a judge on the Audiencia of Mexico) and printed in 1563 by Pedro Ocharte, Mexico's third printer.

FIG. 6. NEW SPAIN, *Ordenanças y copilación de leyes.*

6.

ALPHONSUS, A VERA CRUCE (Fray Alonso de la Vera Cruz) (c. 1504–1584). *Recognitio, summularum.* Mexico, 1554. *Dialectica resolutio.* Mexico, 1554. *Phisica, speculatio.* Mexico, 1557.

Mexico's first printer produced other secular books, including three Latin academic texts either written or edited by the distinguished Augustinian teacher, scholar, and book collector, Fray Alonso de la Vera Cruz. He was the first professor to occupy the chair of scholastic theology at the Royal and Pontifical University of Mexico, having been appointed to that position in 1553, the year in which the institution opened its doors. His *Phisica, speculatio* is believed to be an original work, the first presenting European concepts of physical science to be printed in the Americas. Aristotle's *Dialectica resolutio*, one of two other texts bound in this volume, is the earliest translation of a Classical author's work to be published in the New World (fig. 7). Only two copies of this

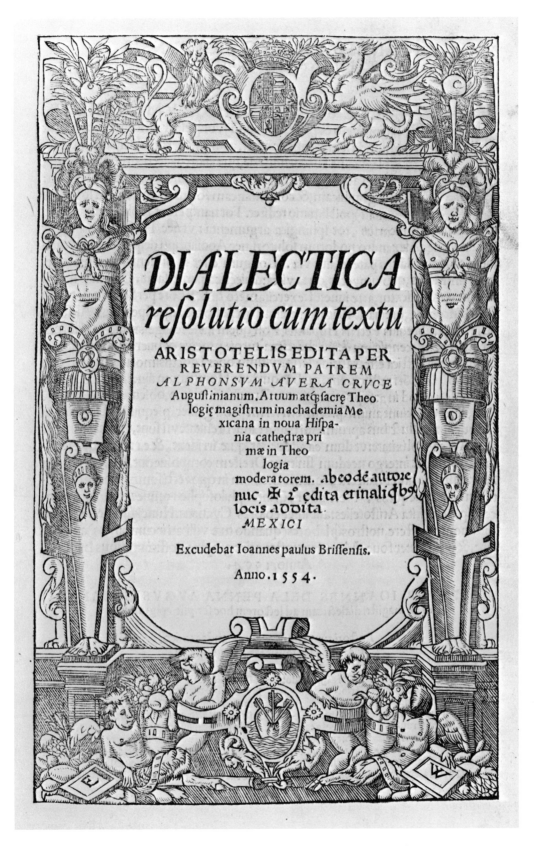

DIALECTICA
resolutio cum textu

ARISTOTELIS EDITA PER
REVERENDVM PATREM
ALPHONSVM AVERA CRVCE
Auguſtinianum, Artium atꝗ ſacrę Theo
logię magiſtrum in achademia Me
xicana in noua Hiſpa-
nia cathedræ pri
mæ in Theo
logia
moderatorem. abeodē autoꝛe
nuc ⳾ 2ᵉ ędita etinalicꝗbꝰ
locis addita.
MEXICI

Excudebat Ioannes paulus Briſſenſis.

Anno. 1 5 5 4.

FIG. 7. ALPHONSUS, A VERA CRUCE, *Dialectica resolutio.*

translated work are recorded in the United States. The marginalia, appearing throughout the John Carter Brown copy, are in the churchman's own hand and contain additions
and corrections made in the subsequent editions published in Salamanca.

7.

BARTOLOMÉ DE LAS CASAS (1474–1566). *Brevissima relacion de la destruycion
de las Indias*. Seville, [1553].

The missionaries who undertook the
evangelization of America's natives were
not only concerned with the spiritual salva-
tion of their converts; they also sought to
protect their physical well-being. After wit-
nessing the abrupt decline in the Caribbean
native population from disease and over-
work, Father Bartolomé de las Casas began
a humanitarian campaign on behalf of the
Church's Indian wards. Because of his
prominent role in this crusade, he was
named "Protector of the Indians" by his
superior, Cardinal Jiménez de Cisneros.

Las Casas wrote his *Brevíssima relación*
(fig. 8) as part of his effort to present a per-
suasive case for the protection of the Indian,
and he therefore focuses entirely upon in-
stances of Spanish cruelty during the conquest. According to Las Casas, tremendous
numbers of native Americans perished at
the hands of the Spaniards, and others were
brutally mutilated. Gruesome descriptions
of the Indians' suffering won the sympathy

FIG. 8. BARTOLOMÉ DE LAS CASAS, *Brevíssima relación*.

of authorities in Spain who then passed legislation abolishing the *encomienda* system,
under which allotments of Indians had been forced to work for the Spaniards.

8.

BARTOLOMÉ DE LAS CASAS (1474–1566). *Narratio regionum indicarum per
Hispanos quosdam devastatarum verissima*. Frankfurt, 1598.

Las Casas's version of Spanish atrocities in the New World had considerable impact on
international politics, and his account was used by Spain's enemies as the basis for the

"black legend" excoriating Spanish cruelty. Editions of the *Brevíssima relación* were translated and published in France, Holland, England, and Germany, some with detailed illustrations of horrifying violence (fig. 9), which helped to justify intervention by other nations in the Western Hemisphere. This Latin edition, published in Frankfurt, is a translation of *Tyrannies et cruautez des Espagnols* (Antwerp, 1579), itself a translation of the *Brevíssima relación*.

FIG. 9. Spanish cruelty, from BARTOLOMÉ DE LAS CASAS, *Narratio regionum*.

Among the shocking scenes depicted in this edition is the massacre of Queen Anacaona and her subjects (fig. 10). After an elaborate reception celebrating the arrival of Nicolás de Ovando (Christopher Columbus's successor as governor of Hispaniola), members of the Queen's entourage were burned alive; in deference to her rank, she was hanged. When word of the incident reached Spain, Queen Isabella herself was among those who expressed their sorrow at the fate of the Indians.

FIG. 10. The death of Queen Anacaona, from BARTOLOMÉ DE LAS CASAS, *Narratio regionum*.

9.

SPAIN. *Leyes y ordenanças nuevame[n]te hechas por Su Magestad, p[ar]a la governacion de las Indias y buen tratamiento y conservacion de los indios.* Alcalá de Henares, 1543.

Influenced by Father Las Casas and other like-minded individuals, the Spanish monarch Charles I issued and sent to the New World an important set of decrees known as the "New Laws of the Indies." According to this document, the *encomienda* was to be phased out gradually with the death of the present owners, and no new allotments of Indians were to be granted.

The laws were not well-received in the colonies. In Mexico, Viceroy Antonio de Mendoza declined to enforce them, and in Peru, Gonzalo Pizarro led a generalized revolt against their implementation.

10.

CATHOLIC CHURCH. *Testerian catechism* (MS). [Mexico, eighteenth century]

Father Jacobo de Testera, a sixteenth-century churchman, wished to create the best possible atmosphere for the rapid conversion of Mexico's natives to the Christian faith. In order to eliminate the need for immediate language training for both Indians and friars, he devised a unique form of picture-writing in which to present religious materials. When the names of the objects depicted were spoken aloud in the indigenous language, the sound approximated that of the Latin words of prayers and portions of the Mass. This manuscript booklet of thirteen leaves (fig. 11) is one of three Testerian catechisms in the John Carter Brown Library.

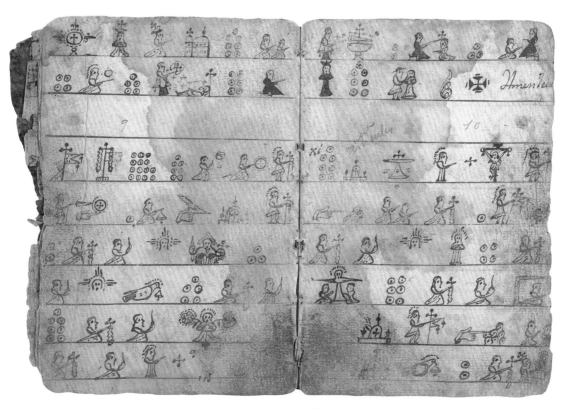

FIG. 11. CATHOLIC CHURCH, *Testerian catechism* (MS).

11.

MATURINO GILBERTI (1498–1585). *Dialogo de doctrina christiana enla lengua d[e] Mechuaca[n]*. Mexico, 1559.

Fray Maturino Gilberti was a colleague of Father Jacobo de Testera and one of the most illustrious Franciscans to dedicate himself to the conversion of Mexico's Indians. Known as the "Cicero of Tarascan" (the Indian language of Michoacán), he wrote numerous works of religious and linguistic importance. His 1558 *Arte de la lengua de Michuacan*, of which the John Carter Brown Library has the only copy in the United States, was the first grammar of an Indian language published in the New World. The publication of his *Diálogo de doctrina christiana* in Tarascan (fig. 12) became enmeshed in questions about the accuracy of the translations, and all copies were confiscated by order of the bishops. Spain's first real *Index* of forbidden books, published the same year as Gilberti's work, warned against the circulation of Christian doctrine in languages other than Latin. Although the Inquisition was not established in Mexico until 1571, this problem would be one of the first to be considered by its judges.

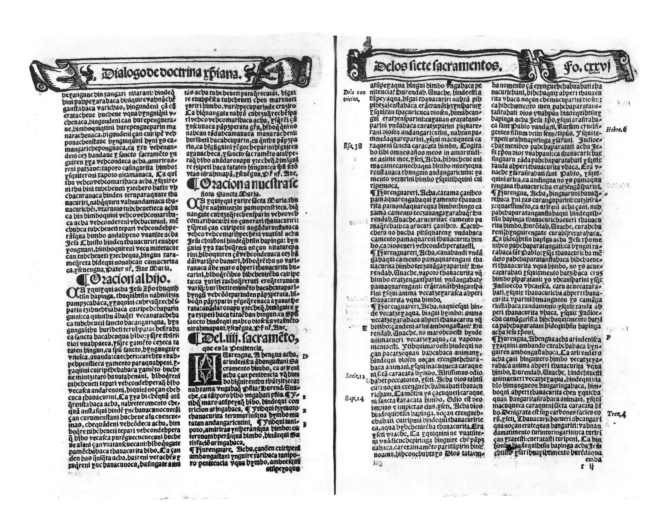

FIG. 12. MATURINO GILBERTI, *Diálogo de doctrina christiana.*

12.

ANTONIO DE CIUDAD REAL (1551–1617). *Maya-Spanish and Spanish-Maya dictionary: the Diccionario de Motul* (MS). [Mexico, after 1577: probably *c.* 1600–1630].

The Mayan civilization, which emerged around 1500 B.C., extended eventually from Yucatan to Western Honduras. A sophisticated architecture, sculpture, painting, mathematics, and astronomy are among the Mayas' cultural and intellectual achievements, and they were responsible as well for devising an early system of writing antedating the European conquest of the Western Hemisphere. At the peak of their civilization, Mayan scribes routinely prepared folded screens of paper made from bark, inscribing them with pictographs and ideographs recording various aspects of their daily life. Believing that these manuscripts were the works of the devil, Cortés and his soldiers destroyed many of them in the first book-burnings carried out by the Spaniards in the New World.

The "Diccionario de Motul" (fig. 13) was compiled to help Spaniards communicate more effectively with the descendants of the great Mayan people. The lexicon demonstrates that the friars used a number of indigenous words having to do with books. Centuries later, it was a source of information for archaeologists who excavated the ruins at Chichén Itzá.

13.

BERNARDINO DE SAHAGÚN (d. 1590). *Psalmodia christiana.* Mexico, 1583.

Another outstanding Franciscan who came to the New World to advance the goals of Indian conversion was Father Bernardino de Sahagún. As a Latin teacher, he began instructing natives at Tlatelolco's Colegio de Santa Cruz in 1536, the year it opened. As a historian, he won acclaim for his *Historia general de las cosas de Nueva España*, which contains a detailed account of the daily life and customs of the Aztecs and other indigenous peoples of Central Mexico. During the course of his missionary duties, he wrote numerous religious works, but only a few were published.

Among Sahagún's *obras* in the John Carter Brown Library is the printed hymnal entitled *Psalmodia christiana* (figs. 14 and 15). It consists of a collection of psalms written in Nahuatl which were to be performed in *areítos* or brief dramatic interludes. As Fray Toribio Motolinía (d. 1568) attests in his *Historia de los indios de la Nueva España*, dramatic representations were an important instructional tool used by the friars in the evangelization of the Indians. The *Psalmodia christiana*, only three copies of which are recorded in the United States, was published by Pedro Ocharte, Mexico's third printer and the son-in-law of Juan Pablos. Because he allegedly praised a work denying the intervention of saints, Ocharte became one of the first victims of the Inquisition in Mexico City.

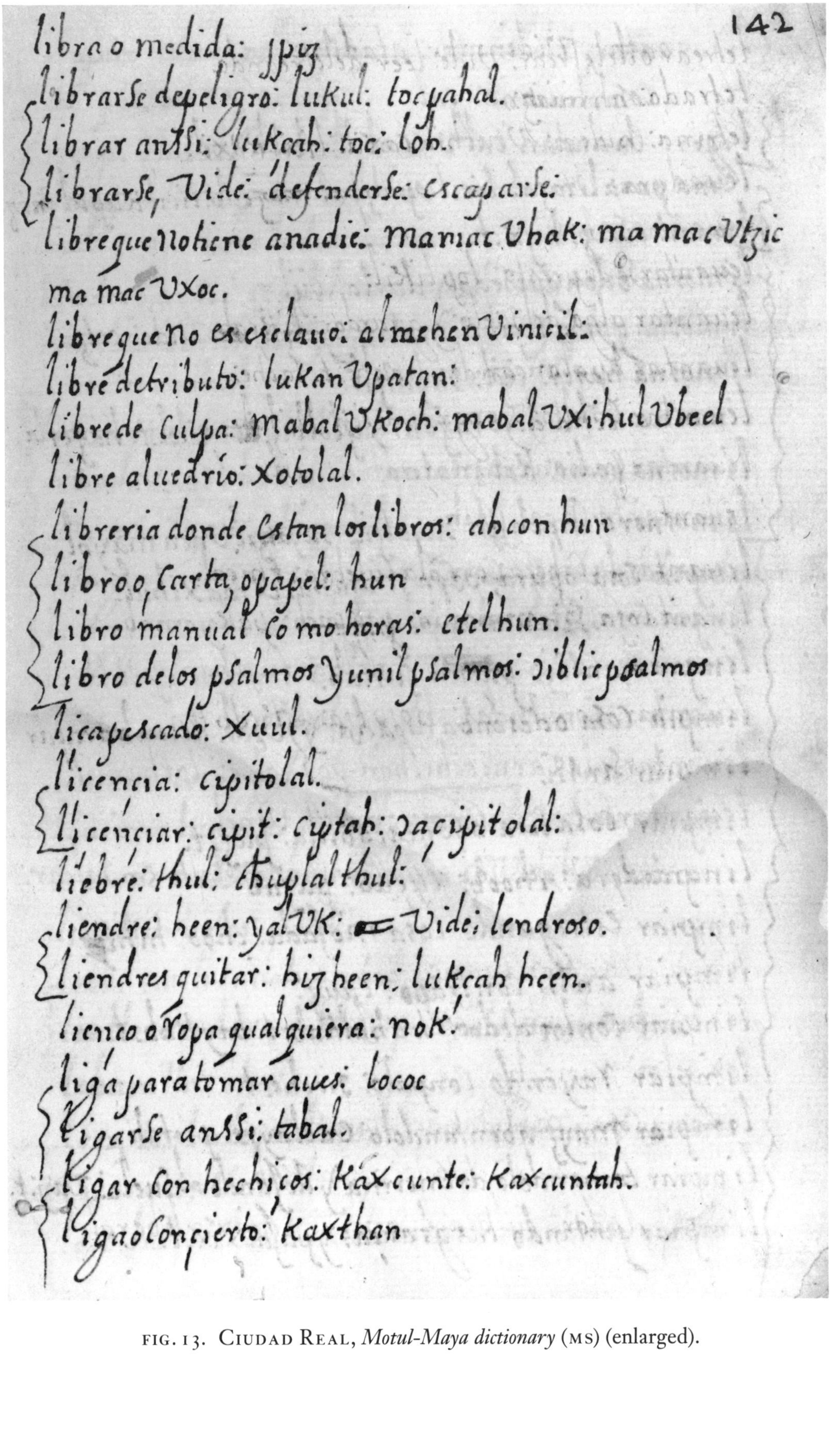

libra o medida: jpiz

{ librarse depeligro: lukul: tocyabal.

{ librar anssi: lukcah: toc: lob.

{ librarse, Vide: defenderse: escayarse.

libre que nohiene anadie: ma mac Vhak: ma mac Vtzic
ma mac Vxoc.

libre que no es esclauo: almehen Vinicil.

libre detributo: lukan Vpatan.

libre de culpa: mabal V koch: mabal Vxihul Vbeel

libre aluedrio: Xotolal.

{ libreria donde estan los libros: ahcon hun

{ libro o carta o papel: hun

{ libro manual como horas: etel hun.

{ libro delos psalmos yunil psalmos: biblie psalmos

Tica pescado: Xuul.

{ licencia: cipitolal.

{ licenciar: cipit: ciptah: bacipitolal.

liebre: thul: ebuplal thul.

liendre: heen: yal VK: Vide: lendroso.

{ liendres quitar: hizheen: lukcah heen.

lienço o ropa qualquiera: nok

liga para tomar aues: lococ

{ ligarse anssi: tabal

{ ligar con hechicos: Kaxcunte: Kaxcuntah.

{ liga o concierto: Kaxthan

FIG. 13. Ciudad Real, *Motul-Maya dictionary* (ms) (enlarged).

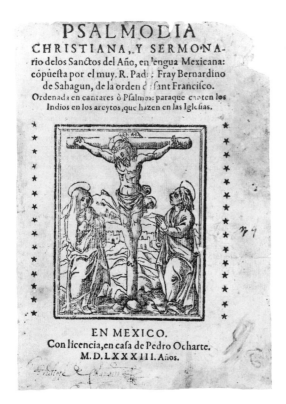

FIG. 14. BERNARDINO DE SAHAGÚN, *Psalmo-dia christiana.*

FIG. 15. The First Psalm, from BERNARDINO DE SAHAGÚN, *Psalmodia christiana.*

14.

JUAN DE TOVAR (*c.* 1546–*c.* 1626). *Historia de la benida de los yndios* (MS). [Mexico, *c.* 1585].

Based upon a history of the Aztecs by the Dominican Diego Durán, Tovar's *Historia de la benida de los yndios* contains detailed information about the rites and ceremonies of the Aztecs, an elaborate comparison of the Aztec year with the Christian calendar, and the correspondence between Tovar and the Jesuit Father José de Acosta. A copy of Tovar's history was sent to Acosta in Peru, and he used it as an important source for his own history of the Indies.

This history appears to be a holograph, and it is illustrated with fifty-one full-page paintings in watercolor. Strongly influenced by Aztec picture-writing, they are of exceptional artistic quality (fig. 16). Among the renderings are representations of Huitzilopochtli (fig. 17), the god of war and principal deity of the Aztecs, and Quetzalcoatl (fig. 18), the Toltec king-god who had been incorporated into the Aztec religious hierarchy. Several of Moctezuma's advisors believed that Hernán Cortés was the peace-

FIG. 16. Hill of the Grasshopper, from JUAN DE TOVAR, *Historia de la benida de los yndios* (MS).

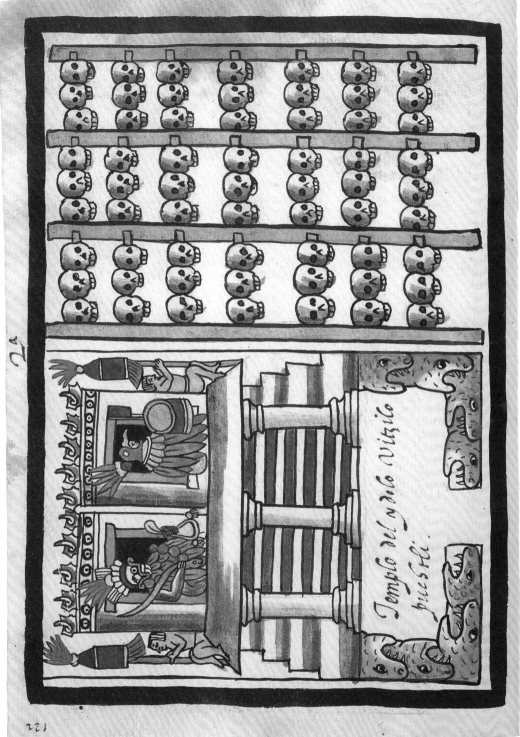

FIG. 17. The temple of Huitzilopochtli, from JUAN DE TOVAR, *Historia de la benida de los yndios* (MS).

Quetzalcoatl
Dios particular
delos de Chulu=
la.

FIG. 18. Quetzalcoatl, from JUAN DE TOVAR, *Historia de la benida de los yndios* (MS).

Quetzalcoatl, who had returned from the East to lead his people as he had promised. The motif of the plumed serpent, Quetzalcoatl's symbol, graces many monuments of the Toltec, Maya, and Aztec civilizations.

15.

NICOLÁS MONARDES (*c.* 1512–1588). *Dos libros. El uno trata de todas las cosas q[ue] trae[n] de n[uest]ras Indias Occide[n]tales, que sirven al uso de medicina.* Seville, 1565.

The natural environment of the New World fascinated early scientists, many of whom came to the Indies during the colonial period. They were particularly intrigued by the unusual vegetation and searched for plants with medicinal properties. After collecting seeds in New Spain and growing them in his garden in Seville, the botanist Nicolás Monardes composed this work on American herbs and drugs, which would constitute a major step in the history of medical science (fig. 19). Although many of the curative agents that he gathered and tested, such as guaiacum wood and the bezar stone, failed to prove effective against Old World diseases, some, like quinine and ipecac, continue to play a role in modern pharmacology. Only three copies of this work are recorded in the United States.

16.

NICOLÁS MONARDES (*c.* 1512–1588). *Joyfull Newes out of the Newe Founde Worlde.* London, 1577.

By the end of the sixteenth century, Monardes's medical treatise had appeared in seventeen different editions in four languages. This English translation was done by John Frampton, and its title is an indication of the enthusiasm with which the botanist's study was received. Frampton, an English merchant, had spent years in a Spanish prison by order of the Inquisition. He allegedly undertook this assignment to interest his own countrymen in tapping the vast wealth of the Americas.

17.

FRANCISCO HERNÁNDEZ (1514–1587). *Quatro libros. De la naturaleza, y virtudes de las plantas, y animales que estan recevidos en el uso de medicina en la Nueva España.* Mexico, 1615.

This abridged and translated version of the medical information contained in Francisco Hernández's twenty-volume Latin manuscript on the natural history of New Spain is the earliest work published in the New World describing the medicinal value of native

DOS LIBROS.

El vno trata de todas las cofas q̃ traẽ de nr̃as Indias Occidẽtales, que firuen al vfo de Medicina, y como fe ha de vfar dela rayz del Mechoacá, purga excelẽtiffima. El otro libro, trata de dos medicinas marauillofas q̃ fon cõtra todo Veneno, la piedra Bezaar, y la yerua Efcuerçonera. Con la cura delos Venenados. Do veran muchos fecretos de naturaleza y de medicina, cõ grãdes experiẽcias. ¶Agora nueuamente cõpueftos por el Doctor Niculofo de Monardes medico de Seuilla. Cõ preuilegio de fu mageftad. 1565.

¶Efta taffado en ̃ ſi — marauedis.

FIG. 19. NICOLÁS MONARDES, *Dos libros* (enlarged).

plants (fig. 20). Hernández was the personal physician of Philip II and was named Protomedicus of New Spain in order to carry out a scientific study of the viceroyalty's plants, animals, and minerals. After his arrival in 1570, he began gathering specimens and testing their various properties. In addition to compiling the results of his experiments, he asked native artists to illustrate his work. The coloring of these illustrations was reported to be of extraordinary quality because of the artists' desire to be as realistic as possible.

FIG. 20. Woodcut and page from FRANCISCO HERNÁNDEZ, *Quatro libros*.

In 1577 Hernández took one completed set of his volumes back to Spain where he hoped to have his work published. Unfortunately, however, the manuscript was simply bound and placed in the library of the Escorial, and the illustrations were hung on the monastery's walls. In the fire of 1671 both the text and the original drawings in color were damaged. Woodcut illustrations, supposedly derived from Hernández's original drawings, appear in Juan Eusebio Nieremberg's *Historia Naturae*, published in Antwerp in 1635 (figs. 21, 22, 23, and 24).

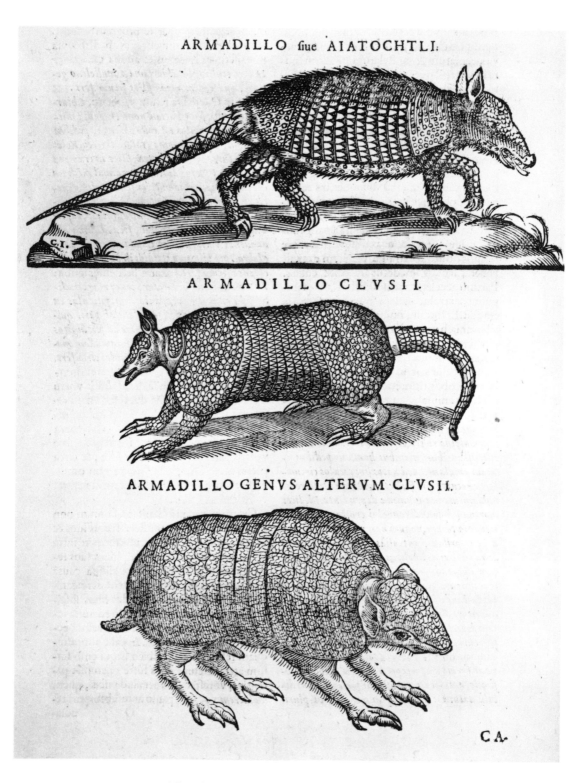

ARMADILLO siue AIATOCHTLI.

ARMADILLO CLVSII.

ARMADILLO GENVS ALTERVM CLVSII.

FIG. 21. Armadillos, from JUAN EUSEBIO NIEREMBERG, *Historia naturae*.

(26)

VICVNA.

TVNA, SIVE NOPALLI
SAXIS INNASCENS.

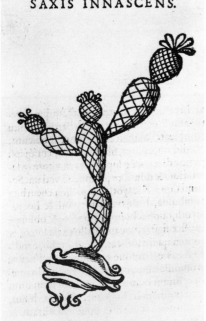

TEOAMATL, VITÆ ET MORTIS INDEX.

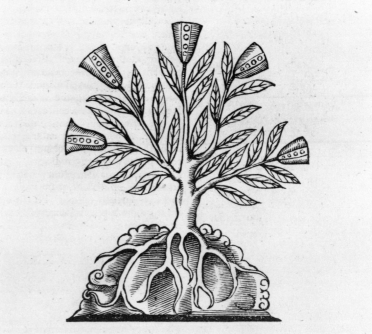

FIG. 22. Vicuña, from JUAN EUSEBIO NIEREMBERG, *Historia naturae.*

FIG. 23. Cactus plant with fruit, from JUAN EUSEBIO NIEREMBERG, *Historia naturae.*

FIG. 24. Teoamatl plant, from JUAN EUSEBIO NIEREMBERG, *Historia naturae.*

18.

MATEO ALEMÁN (1547–after 1615). *Ortografía castellana*. Mexico, 1609.

A number of Spanish writers were attracted to the New World, and they wrote and published their works throughout the colonies. Among them was Mateo Alemán, author of the famous picaresque novel *Guzmán de Alfarache*. In 1599 the first part of this masterpiece was published in Madrid and enjoyed more immediate success than Cervantes's *Don Quijote*.

In an effort to protect newly-converted Indians from frivolity, the Spanish crown at first sought to prohibit the importation and publication of works of pure fiction such as *Guzmán de Alfarache*. Although initially banned from the Americas, the *Guzmán* was shipped to the New World in quantity during the early years of the seventeenth century, according to extant ship manifests.

Works of instruction were more acceptable than novels, and the authorities readily permitted Alemán's treatise on peninsular orthography (fig. 25) to be produced by the family of Mexico's fourth printer, Pedro Balli. By the time Alemán published more of his writings, Balli's widow, Catalina del Valle, was in charge of the business. In the Spanish American colonies, the widows of printers often assumed entrepreneurial duties. In Mexico, the tradition was begun in 1594 by María de Sansoric, who began work on the printing of Father Manuel Alvarez's *De institutione grammatica* after the death of her husband, Pedro Ocharte.

FIG. 25. MATEO ALEMÁN, *Ortografía castellana*.

19.

MATEO ALEMÁN (1547–after 1615). *Sucesos de D. frai García Gera arcobispo de Mejico*. Mexico, 1613.

On August 9, 1608, Fray García Guerra (1560–1612) arrived at the port of Veracruz to assume his position as Archbishop of the New World's wealthiest see, and in 1611 he became Viceroy of New Spain as well. The major events of his tragically short tenure as Archbishop-Viceroy were documented in this account by Mateo Alemán, who accompanied the eminent Dominican to the Indies (fig. 26).

LEGENDO SIMVLQVE PERAGRANDO.

FIG. 26. Portrait of Alemán, from MATEO ALEMÁN, *Sucesos de d. frai García Gera* (enlarged).

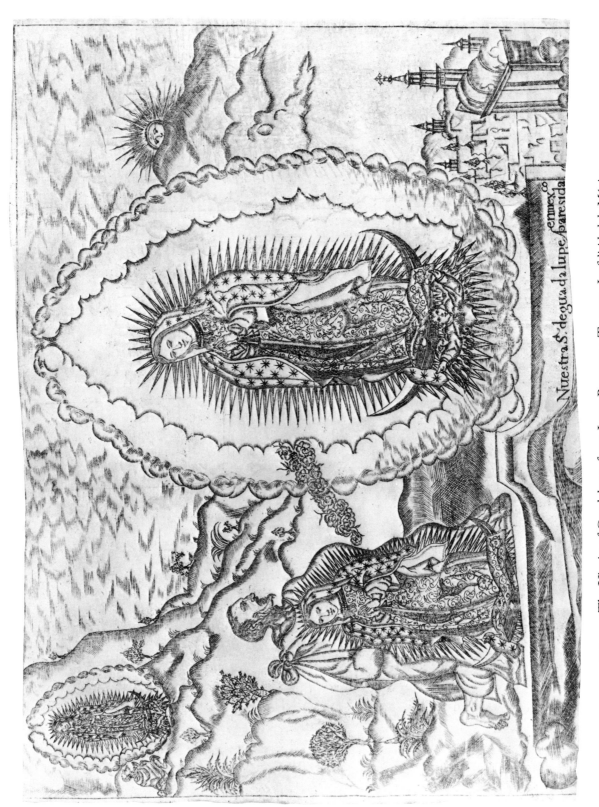

Nuestra S. de gua. d'lupe en mex. paresida

FIG. 27. The Virgin of Guadalupe, from LUIS BECERRA TANCO, *La felicidad de México.*

When Alemán arrived in the New World, his copy of *Don Quijote* was confiscated by inspectors of the Holy Office of the Inquisition. Such measures, however, did not stop the flow of creative and imaginative works to the colonies, and Alemán's book was later returned to him.

Only two copies of Alemán's account of Fray García Guerra's residence in Mexico are recorded in the United States.

20.

Luis Becerra Tanco (1602–1672). *Felicidad de Mexico*. Mexico, 1675.

The Virgin of Guadalupe, whose apparition aided sixteenth-century friars in the conversion of Mexico's Indians, became increasingly popular as an object of adoration throughout the colonial period. Early in the nineteenth century, revolutionary forces rallied around her image, and she is a contemporary symbol of the country's religious devotion. In his *Felicidad de México*, Luis Becerra Tanco describes the circumstances surrounding the miraculous appearance of the Virgin with Indian features and the efforts of Juan Diego, a native laborer, to fulfill her request by having a shrine built in her honor. Juan Diego reportedly experienced her presence on the hill of Tepeyac near the site of the temple to the Aztec goddess Tonantzin. Bishop Zumárraga was reluctant to believe Juan Diego's story but finally accepted his mantle with the Madonna's semblance on it as proof of her divine intervention.

The portrait of the Virgin of Guadalupe was duplicated many times by early Mexican printers. This particular one (fig. 27), influenced more by European artistic traditions than by native American images, was the nineteenth known to have been printed in Mexico. It is eloquent testimony to the capacity of printers and engravers in seventeenth-century New Spain to produce excellent work.

Only two copies of this book, the second edition, are recorded in the United States. The first edition appeared in 1666 under a different title.

21.

Eusebio Francisco Kino (1644–1711). *Exposicion astronomica de el cometa*. Mexico, 1681.

22.

Carlos de Sigüenza y Góngora (1645–1700). *Libra astronomica*. Mexico, 1690.

The great comet, which appeared over New Spain in 1680–1681, sparked an intense controversy between the Tyrolean Jesuit, Father Eusebio Francisco Kino, and the Creole savant, Don Carlos de Sigüenza y Góngora, over its significance for New World

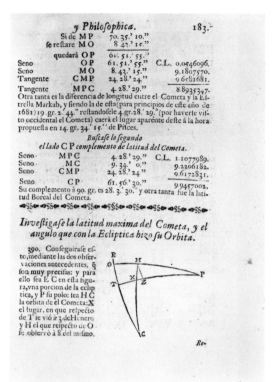

FIG. 28. EUSEBIO FRANCISCO KINO, *Exposición astronómica*.

FIG. 29. Observations of the comet, from CAR-LOS DE SIGÜENZA Y GÓNGORA, *Libra astronómica*.

residents. Their arguments constitute the first intellectual debate to appear in print in the Indies over a matter of scientific importance based on local experience. The clash is symbolic also of the ongoing conflict between superstition and science.

Father Kino, later a well-known missionary and explorer of northwestern New Spain, held the traditional view that the comet was an ominous warning of divine origin, sent by God to announce His displeasure and to foretell punishment (fig. 28). Don Carlos de Sigüenza y Góngora opposed Father Kino's obscurantist interpretation and sought to dispel the fear surrounding the occurrence by gathering scientific information about the comet itself.

As an outstanding intellectual, Sigüenza reportedly had been invited to the French court of Louis XIV, but he declined in order to occupy the chair of astrology and mathematics at Mexico's university. His erudite *Libra astronómica*, which includes observations made by him from January 3 to January 20, 1681 (fig. 29), is indicative of the high level of European scientific scholarship produced in Spanish America.

The copy of *Libra astronómica* in the John Carter Brown Library was once in the collection of the Colegio de San Juan, as the brand on the bottom edge of the volume indicates (fig. 30). Many books were marked this way during the colonial period, and the markings yield valuable information about the extent of the holdings of early libraries in the New World.

FIG. 30. Book brand of the Colegio de San Juan, from CARLOS DE SIGÜENZA Y GÓNGORA, *Libra astronómica*.

23.

SISTER JUANA INÉS DE LA CRUZ (1648–1695). *Villancicos*. Mexico, [1677].

Sor Juana Inés de la Cruz, whose brilliant literary career as poet, prose writer, and playwright won her the title of the "Tenth Muse," composed numerous poems for religious festivities in Mexico. Among them are her *villancicos* or church carols sung on Catholic feast or saints' days. Although the musical notations for these pieces were not recorded, the lyrics were printed especially for the occasion. When they published *villancicos*, printers usually followed the small quarto format and placed a woodcut of the Virgin or the saint being honored on the title page (fig. 31). This particular song, written in praise of Saint Peter, is a blend of elements of Mexican culture with aspects of Catholic ritual. In the "Enzalada," one of the composition's intercalated poems, a mestizo comes forth to express his sentiments toward this holy man (fig. 32).

No other copy of the *villancico* to Saint Peter is known to be in the United States.

24.

SISTER JUANA INÉS DE LA CRUZ (1648–1695). *Carta athenagorica*. Puebla de los Angeles, 1690.

In 1690 Sor Juana wrote an eloquent and erudite challenge to a sermon delivered many years earlier by the Portuguese Jesuit, Antonio Vieira. Her rebuttal came to the attention of Puebla's Bishop, Don Manuel Fernández de Santa Cruz, who was so impressed by her scholarship that he had it published under the title *Carta Athenagórica* (fig. 33). The correspondence that accompanied the printed copy sent to Sor Juana praised her for this intellectual achievement but criticized her for not devoting her energy exclusively to religious endeavors.

Months after Sor Juana received the Bishop's letter, she responded to his criticism

VILLANCICOS,
QVE SE CANTARON EN LA SANTA

Iglesia Cathedral de Mexico, à los Maytines del Gloriosissimo Principe de la
Iglesia, el Señor SAN PEDRO.

Que fundò, y dotò el Doct. y M. D. Simon Estevan Beltran, de Alzate, y Esquibel (que
Dios aya) Maestre-escuela, que fue, desta S. Iglesia Cathedral, y Cathedratico Jubilado de
Sagrada Escriptura, en esta Real Universidad de Mexico.

Año de 1677.

DEDICALOS,

AL Señor Lic.do D. Garcia de Legaspi, Velazco, Altamirano, y
Albornoz, Canonigo desta Santa Iglesia Cathedral de Mexico, &c.

Señor mio, ofrezcole à V. Señoria, los Villancicos, que para los Maitines del Principe de los Apostoles S. Pedro, hize como pude à violencias de mi esteril vena, po-
ca cultura, corta salud, y menos lugar, por las indispensables ocupaciones de mi
estado. Lo festivo de sus alegorias se debe à la fiesta; y sobre el comun privilegio de
versos, tienen ampla licencia en la imitacion de mi gran P. S. Geronimo, que en vna
Epistola ad Eustochium dize: *Festus est dies, & natalis Beati Petri festivius est solito con-
diendus, ita tamen, vt scripturarum cardinem iocularis sermo non fugiat.* Lo que tienen
de malos sanar puede à la sombra de Pedro; aunque he advertido, que para sanar el mal
de vnos pies (tal es el mas incurable de los versos) se valiò de su mano: imagen, y viva
sombra de sus padres son los hijos, que con la imitacion de sus exemplos sino igualan, à
lo menos siguen el tamaño de sus virtudes, y grandeza de sus hazañas: sealo U. Señoria
de su P. S. Pedro, por lo Ecclesiastico, ya que en lo natural, y politico es glorioso es-
plendor de sus nobilissimos progenitores, y dè la mano de su favor à mis versos, para
que corran como buenos à la sombra de su patrocinio: para conseguirla no alego mas
titulos porque no quiero adelantarle à U. Señoria en el rostro el color, que desea la
purpura en sus vestidos ambiciosa de reteñirse en el Capelo con el lustre, y honor de
su sangre. Tampoco escusò la pequeñes de lo que ofrezco, porque como hija de S. Geronimo, quiero que U. Señoria la escuse con sus palabras, en la Epistola ad Marcellam,
reconociendo en lo pequeño del don, lo consagrado de la voluntad, q̃ lo ofrece: *Quia
velata Virginis munus est, aliqua in ipsis munusculis esse misteria demonstremus.* Guarde
Dios à U. Señoria como deseo. Es deste Convento de N. P. S. Geronymo, Junio 20.
de 1677. años.

B. L. M. D. U. Señoria, su mas afecta servidora, que mas le estima.

Juana Ines de la Cruz.

FIG. 31. Woodcut of Saint Peter, from SOR JUANA INÉS DE LA CRUZ, *Villancicos* (enlarged).

(34)

al gallinaço venciendo.
Era Malco vn miferable,
    y compafivo de verlo,
quifo darle heridas *francas*,
    pues no le daba dineros.
No le pudo fu contrario
    ofender en vn cabello,
porque acertò en la pendencia,
    à proporcionar el *medio*.
Mas llegando al eftrechar
    vna moçuela riñendo
con flaqueça fobre fuerça,
    le hizo perder fus alientos,
Hiriole en lo mas fenfible;
    mas que mucho, fi perdiendo
la *rectitud*, fue precifo
    dexar fin defenfa el cuerpo.
Mas haziendo al mifmo punto
    de *conclufion* movimiento
de fuprema dignidad
    gozò fu *treta* los fueros.

✠ II. ✠
❧ ENZALADA. ❧
Introduccion.

EN el dia de SAN PEDRO,
    por grandeza de fus llaves,
como es fiefta de Portero,
    fe da la entrada de valde.
Con aquefta ocafion, pues,
    entraron à celebrarle
de lo meior de los Barrios
    multitud de perfonajes.
El primero fu vn Meftizo,
    que con vozes arrogantes
le difparò eftos elogios,
    disfraçados en corage.   *Gloffas.*
Oy es el feñor SAN PEDRO,
    que fue la piedra de Chrifto,
y allà en el huerto orejano
    fe hizo de piedra, y cuchillo.

Y no fue mucho milagro,
    que moftrafe tantos brios,
pues del barrio de San Juan,
    fe dize, que era vezino.
Cobrò con aquefto fama
    de tan valiente, y temido,
que le ayunao las Vigilias.
    hafta fus amigos mifmos
Eftuvo preffo vna vez
    con tan cercano peligro,
que librarfe de la muerte
    fue milagro conocido.
Por aquefto, y otras cofas
    por guardar el individuo,
ganò la Iglefia, y en ella
    fue perpetuo retraydo.
Efto fue en fu mocedad,
    que defpues fue Dios fervido,
que muriò como vn Apoftol,
    mas fin dexar el oficio.

Profigue la introduccion.

Defpues defte, vn Portugues
    preciado de navegante,
como era ya hombre à la mar,
    quifo à los mares echarfe.
Y mirando en alta mar
    de PEDRO la hermofa nave,
por ayudarla con foplos
    echò fus coplas al ayre.

❧ COPLAS. ❧

Timoneyro, que governas
    la Nave do el Evangelio,
è los tefouros da Igrexa
    van â tua maun fugeitos.
Mide â equinociales grados,
    è de ò Sol ò apartamento,
pois en todo ò mundo tein
    de fervir tuo deroteiro.
Ollai, que por muita altura

per.

FIG. 32. "Enzalada," from SOR JUANA INÉS DE LA CRUZ, *Villancicos* (enlarged).

(35)

FIG. 33. Sor Juana Inés de la Cruz, *Carta athenagórica*.

in her now famous *Respuesta a Sor Filotea de la Cruz*. In this reply, she traces the development of her "inclination toward study" to her childhood when she learned to read at the age of three, won her first prize in a poetry competition five years later, and dreamed of attending the Royal and Pontifical University of Mexico. This institution of higher learning was closed to women, however, and even Sor Juana's offer to dress like a man could not gain her admission. In her youth, before she became a nun, she had been a member of the viceregal court and had written many secular works for her illustrious admirers. Because her *Respuesta* also contains a defense of women's right to intellectual freedom, Sor Juana is often considered to be America's first feminist.

25.

Coyoacán codex (MS). [Mexico, c. 1700 – before 1743].

Pictorial manuscripts using indigenous techniques were still being made two hundred years after the conquest, and some were prepared as forgeries of original titles to property. This codex of fourteen leaves (figs. 34 and 35), usually classified as belonging to the Techialoyan group of writings, is a land claim prepared by residents of Mazatepe, an Indian village whose boundaries were being challenged by the authorities. By using native *amatl* paper derived from fig tree bark, and by combining watercolor paintings with glosses written in Nahuatl, the forgers endeavored to imitate sixteenth-century documentation of landholdings.

26.

Hernán Cortés (1485–1547). *Historia de Nueva-España . . . aumentada con otros documentos, y notas, por el ilustrissimo señor don Francisco Antonio Lorenzana. . . . Mexico, 1770.*

Francisco Antonio de Lorenzana y Buitrón (1722–1804) was among the most brilliant clerics to serve as Archbishop of Mexico, a post that he occupied from 1766 to 1772.

Before returning to the Iberian peninsula, he amassed an important collection of manuscripts relative to New Spain, housed today in Toledo's Biblioteca Pública. Among his
many contributions to New Spain's history is this edition of the letter-reports of Cortés,
which also contains records of tribute paid by various Mexican settlements to Moctezuma, and an account of the voyage of Cortés to California in 1535.

Typographically, the *Historia de Nueva-España* is one of the finest products of the
press of Joseph Antonio de Hogal (1766–1787), and it is particularly notable for its
excellent copper engravings. The map of New Spain (fig. 36), view of the Great Temple
of Mexico (fig. 37), frontispiece (fig. 38), and Domingo de Castillo's map of California
were executed by José Mariano Navarro, an engraver and binder of Mexico City. Manuel
de Villavicencio produced the Mexican calendar (fig. 39) and thirty-one plates depicting
the tributes paid to Moctezuma (figs. 40 and 41).

27.

CATHOLIC CHURCH. *Missa Gothica seù Mozarabica*. Puebla de los Angeles
[Mexico], 1770.

Among the earliest imprints of the Real Seminario Palafoxiana of Puebla is the *Missa
Góthica*, a *tour de force* of graphic arts dedicated by the Bishop of Puebla, Francisco Fabián
y Fuero, to his godson, Francisco Antonio de Lorenzana y Buitrón. The Mozarabic rite
of the Mass was authorized in the fifteenth century by the Cardinal Primate of Spain
and Archbishop of Toledo, Francisco Jiménez de Cisneros, for use only in certain
churches in the city of Toledo by those Christians who had been captives during the
Moslem occupation. The publication of this liturgy in New Spain, however, did not
authorize its use there. The work is notable for its beautiful red and black title page and
for its five extraordinarily fine copper engravings (figs. 42, 43, and 44). The latter were
executed by José de Nava, a native of Puebla (1735–1817), who was considered one of
the finest engravers of his time. Apart from its physical beauty, this book is of historical
interest as one of the few surviving texts of this rare and restricted rite of the Mass.

28.

MEXICO. *Decreto constitucional para la libertad de la America mexicana: sancionado
en Apatzingan à 22 de octubre de 1814*. Apatzingán, [1814].

LENT BY THE SUTRO LIBRARY, SAN FRANCISCO.

Although the movement for independence in New Spain was begun by Father Miguel
Hidalgo y Costilla at Dolores in 1810, a concrete plan for an independent state was not
formulated until 1813. At that time, the Acta de Independencia was drawn up and signed
at Chilpancingo. A constitutional congress then drafted an organic law for the creation
of a new nation. The twenty-two articles of the *Decreto constitucional* established a
Catholic, egalitarian, and sovereign state free to elect the form of government most

FIG. 34. *Coyoacán codex* (MS).

FIG. 35. *Coyoacán codex* (MS).

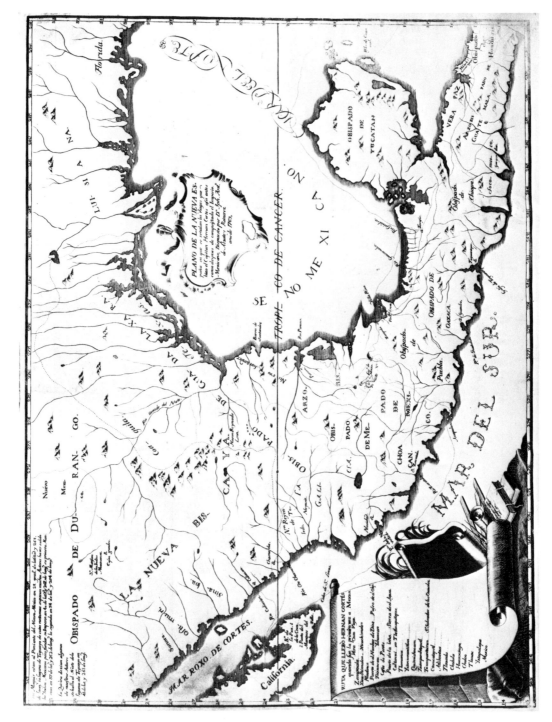

FIG. 36. Map of New Spain, from HERNÁN CORTÉS, *Historia de Nueva España*.

FIG. 37. The Great Temple of Mexico, from HERNÁN CORTÉS, *Historia de Nueva España.*

FIG. 38. Cortés and the King of Spain, from Hernán Cortés, *Historia de Nueva España*.

(42)

FIG. 39. The Veytia calendar wheel, from HERNÁN CORTÉS, *Historia de Nueva España.*

FIG. 40. Indian tribute, from HERNÁN CORTÉS, *Historia de Nueva España*.

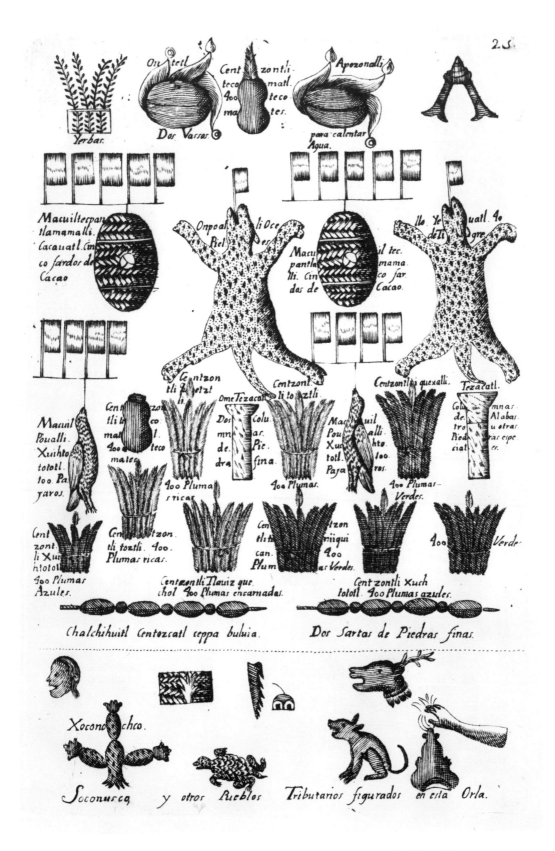

FIG. 41. Indian tribute, from HERNÁN CORTÉS, *Historia de Nueva España*.

(45)

FIG. 42. Engraving, from the *Missa Góthica*.

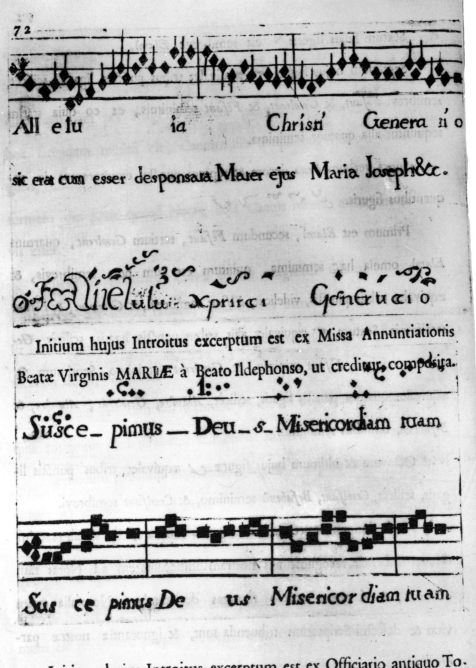

All e lu ia Christi Genera ti o

sic erat cum esset desponsata Mater ejus Maria Joseph &c.

Initium hujus Introitus excerptum est ex Missa Annuntiationis

Beatæ Virginis MARIÆ à Beato Ildephonso, ut creditur, composita.

Susce_pimus _ Deu_s_ Misericordiam tuam

Sus ce pimus De us Misericor diam tu am

Initium hujus Introitus excerptum est ex Officiario antiquo To-
letano *in Festo Purificationis Beatæ Virginis MARIÆ* cum
Cantu prout superiùs ponitur, & æquivalet Notis inferiùs positis.

BRE-

FIG. 43. Musical arrangement, from the *Missa Góthica*.

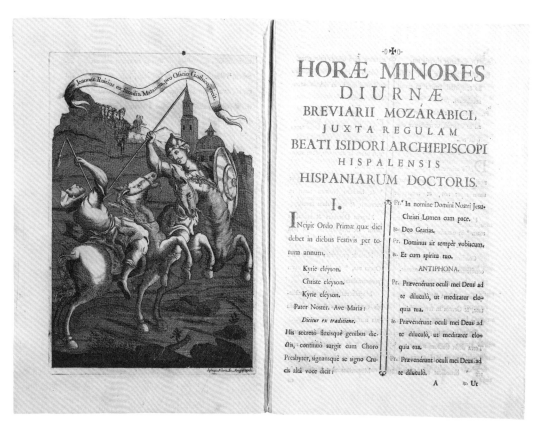

FIG. 44. *Missa Góthica.*

suited to its citizens. Military pressure by royalist troops forced the constitutional congress and its press to move from place to place throughout the modern states of southern Michoacán and northern Guerrero. Finally, at Apatzingán on October 22, 1814, the Constitution was signed by José María Liceaga, José María Morelos, José María Cos, and Remigio de Yarza.

The printed copy of the Constitution from the Sutro Library, dated October 24, 1814, includes the *rúbricas* (individual flourishes similar to initials) of the four signers (fig. 45). It is the only copy reported to be held by a collection outside of Mexico.

THE CAPTAINCY-GENERAL OF GUATEMALA

29.

MANUEL LOBO (1612–1686). *Relacion de la vida, y virtudes del V. hermano Pedro de San Ioseph Betancur.* Guatemala, 1667.

In 1660, at the insistence of Guatemala's Bishop, Fray Payo Enríquez de Ribera, Joseph de Pineda Ibarra (1629–1680) moved his printing press from Puebla de los Angeles near por Tecpan.—Dr. José Maria Cos, diputado por Zacatecas.—Lic. José Sotero de Castañeda, diputado por Durango.—Lic. Cornelio Ortiz de Zarate, diputado por Tlaxcala.—Lic. Manuel de Aldrete y Soria, diputado por Querétaro.—Antonio José Moctezuma, diputado por Coahuila.—Lic. José Maria Ponce de Leon, diputado por Sonora.—Dr. Francisco Argandar, diputado por San Luis Potosí.—Remigio de Yarza, secretario.—Pedro José Bermeo, secretario.

Por tanto: para su puntual observancia publíquese, y circulese à todos los tribunales, justicias, gefes, gobernadores, y demas autoridades asi civiles como militares, y eclesiàsticas de cualquiera clase y dignidad, para que guarden, y hagan guardar, cumplir y executar el presente DECRETO constitucional en todas sus partes.

Palacio nacional del Supremo Gobierno Mexicano en Apatzingan, veinte y cuatro de octubre de mil ochocientos catorce. Año quinto de la independencia mexicana.

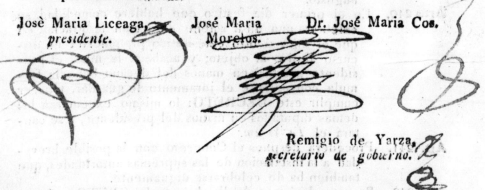

Josè Maria Liceaga, presidente.   José Maria Morelos.   Dr. José Maria Cos.

Remigio de Yarza, secretario de gobierno.

NOTA. Los Exmôs. Srês. Lic. D. Ignacio López Rayon, Lic. D. Manuel Sabino Crespo, Lic. D. Andres Quintana, Lic. D. Carlos Maria de Bustamante, D. Antonio de Sesma, aunque contribuyeron con sus luces à la formacion de este DECRETO, no pudieron firmarlo por estar ausentes al tiempo de la sancion, enfermos unos, y otros empleados en diferentes asuntos del servicio de la Patria.

Yarza.

FIG. 45. Signature flourishes, *Decreto constitucional* (Apatzingán, Mexico).

Mexico City to Central America. The printer's son eventually took over the family business, which would remain Guatemala's sole publishing house until 1714. This example of Pineda Ibarra's work is the only known complete copy of Manuel Lobo's account of Brother Betancur's efforts to convert the Indians of Guatemala and to establish the Convalescent Hospital of Our Lady of Bethlehem in Guatemala City.

30.

DIEGO SÁENZ OVECURI. *Thomasiada al sol de la iglesia, y su doctor santo Thomas de Aquino*. Guatemala, 1667.

Diego Sáenz Ovecuri's book-length poem, also printed by Pineda Ibarra, is believed to be the earliest literary work printed in Central America. In addition to being a poetic biography of St. Thomas Aquinas, the *Thomasiada* contains a treatise on the art of writing poetry (fig. 46). Only two copies of his work are known to be in the United States.

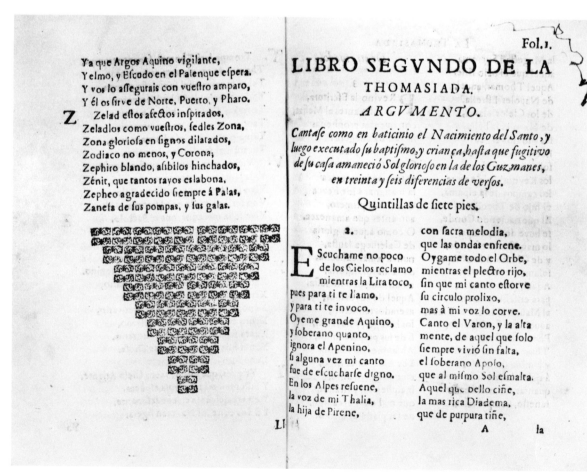

FIG. 46. DIEGO SÁENZ OVECURI, *Thomasiada*.

31.

Noticia del establecimiento del museo de esta capital de la Nueva Guatemala. [Guatemala], 1797.

This museum booklet, printed for the institution's opening, contains information about its establishment, the arrangement of its collection, and the inaugural address delivered on that occasion (fig. 47). According to the description, the museum housed the rare collection made by the naturalist José Longinos Martínez. The naturalist had been sent by Charles IV to replace the specimens gathered by Francisco Hernández that had been damaged by the 1671 fire in the Escorial.

Juana Martínez Batres, the widow of Sebastián de Arévalo, printed this booklet in the shop she inherited from him. She is credited with bringing three additional European presses to Guatemala during her management of the business. Her late husband had made significant contributions to printing by creating fonts that conformed to the Indian alphabet invented by Francisco de la Parra, and by publishing the *Gaceta de Guatemala*, the region's first newspaper, from 1729 to 1731.

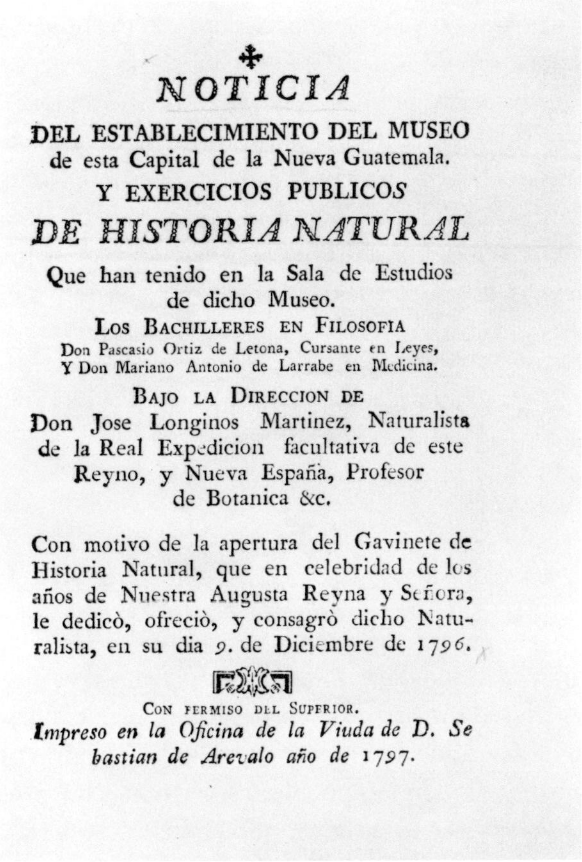

✠
NOTICIA
DEL ESTABLECIMIENTO DEL MUSEO
de esta Capital de la Nueva Guatemala.
Y EXERCICIOS PUBLICOS
DE HISTORIA NATURAL
Que han tenido en la Sala de Estudios
de dicho Museo.
LOS BACHILLERES EN FILOSOFIA
Don Pascasio Ortiz de Letona, Cursante en Leyes,
Y Don Mariano Antonio de Larrabe en Medicina.
BAJO LA DIRECCION DE
Don Jose Longinos Martinez, Naturalista
de la Real Expedicion facultativa de este
Reyno, y Nueva España, Profesor
de Botanica &c.

Con motivo de la apertura del Gavinete de Historia Natural, que en celebridad de los años de Nuestra Augusta Reyna y Señora, le dedicò, ofreciò, y consagrò dicho Naturalista, en su dia 9. de Diciembre de 1796.

CON PERMISO DEL SUPERIOR.
Impreso en la Oficina de la Viuda de D. Sebastian de Arevalo año de 1797.

FIG. 47. *Noticia del establecimiento del museo.*

The Viceroyalty of Peru

THE AUDIENCIA OF LIMA

FRONTISPIECE

FRANCISCO DE XEREZ (b. 1500). *Verdadera relacion de la conquista del Peru.* Seville, 1534.

On November 16, 1532, Spanish troops led by Francisco Pizarro entered the town of Cajamarca, Peru, to confront the Inca ruler Atahualpa and his subjects. The encounter is symbolic of the meeting of two worlds that had already taken place in Mexico and Central America and would soon be repeated throughout the South American continent. Pizarro's secretary, Francisco de Xerez or Jerez, who was present at the time, offers a detailed description of the scene in his *Verdadera relación de la conquista del Perú*, one of the earliest accounts of the Spaniards' conquest of the Inca empire.

An unknown European artist, drawing realistic elements from Xerez's description and blending them with his own ideas about the New World, designed a woodcut for the first edition of the *Verdadera relación*. On the title page, Atahualpa holds what appears to be the Bible that was given to him by Fray Vicente de Valverde. Rejecting the incursion of foreigners into his kingdom and unaware of the importance of the sacred book, Atahualpa threw the Bible to the ground. The military clash that followed—and those provoked by similar encounters throughout the New World—changed forever the character of New World culture.

32.

PEDRO DE CIEZA DE LEÓN (1518–1560). *Parte primera dela chronica del Peru.* Seville, 1553.

Early chroniclers, who witnessed the subjugation of Peru, wrote about the vast kingdom of Tawantinsuyo and offered the first European view of Inca civilization. Accounts such as this one by Pedro de Cieza de León contain valuable information about one of the world's most successful empires and its people, a story that is only suggested by surviving artifacts. Unlike the Mayans, the Incas never developed a system of writing, and knotted cords or *quipus* were the only formal means of making records.

This autograph copy of Cieza's chronicle is distinguished by its unusual woodcuts, which depict a European vision of America sometimes enhanced by fantastic elements. In one of them, the devil, believed to be hard at work in the New World, is shown as he keeps the inhabitants from leading a virtuous Christian life (fig. 48), and in another, Lake Titicaca, located on the desolate Andean *altiplano*, looks curiously like a canal in the city of Venice (fig. 49). The illustration of the Cerro de Potosí (fig. 50), the fabled "silver mountain" of the Indies, is an exception. Because it was based on an original drawing done by the chronicler himself, it more accurately depicts the real place.

FIG. 48. The Devil in the New World, from PEDRO DE
CIEZA DE LEÓN, *Chrónica del Perú* (enlarged).

33.

SPAIN. *Pragmatica sobre los diez dias del año*. Ciudad de los Reyes [Lima], 1584.

In 1580 the Italian printer Antonio Ricardo (d. 1605) left New Spain after a ten-year stay to establish the first printing press in Peru. He had been Mexico's fifth printer and the producer of at least thirteen books in the viceroyalty's capital. As the former partner of Pedro Ocharte, he owned much of the equipment used in their business, and with this he planned to set up shop in Lima. Whether Ricardo decided to move his press to Peru at the request of the Jesuits, in anticipation of the demand for books at the University of San Marcos, or in an effort to benefit from the prestige and affluence of

FIG. 49. Lake Titicaca, from
PEDRO DE CIEZA DE LEÓN,
Chrónica del Perú (enlarged).

FIG. 50. Cerro de Potosí, from
PEDRO DE CIEZA DE LEÓN,
Chrónica del Perú.

viceregal Lima, his printing establishment was opposed by the authorities there, and he was unable to begin operating until 1584.

Ricardo's first publication was to have been *Doctrina christiana*. That project was interrupted, however, when word was received from Europe that Pope Gregory XIII had promulgated a change in the calendar requiring a one-time addition of ten days to the year. Europeans had observed the Gregorian calendar since 1582, and Ricardo's *Pragmática* announced its adoption to Spanish Americans.

The *Pragmática*, a document of only four pages (figs. 51 and 52), was discovered among a group of other Peruvian pamphlets by George Parker Winship, Librarian of the John Carter Brown Library from 1904 to 1915. Close investigation revealed to Winship the extraordinary importance of the *Pragmática*, and in 1912 he published a study in which he concluded that it antedated the 1584 trilingual edition of the *Doctrina christiana*. This conclusion was later confirmed by José Toribio Medina. Only two copies of the work are known to have survived.

34.

CATHOLIC CHURCH. *Tercero cathecismo y exposicion de la doctrina christiana*. Ciudad de los Reyes [Lima], 1585.

The Jesuit Father José de Acosta (1539–1616) presided over Lima's first Provincial Council, a meeting called in 1576 to evaluate the progress of Christian evangelization in Peru. Books, especially vocabularies, grammars, and catechisms in indigenous languages, were urgently needed by members of all the religious orders participating in the Council, and a request for a printer may have been a direct result of the proceedings. When Antonio Ricardo arrived, therefore, his principal duty was to print materials for proselytizing the Indians, and his earliest publications were closely supervised by Father Acosta. The Jesuit, who had become an expert in Andean languages, collaborated with the anonymous churchmen who wrote the first religious works produced on Ricardo's press. Father Acosta personally checked volumes such as the *Tercero cathecismo* for accuracy, and his signature is the mark of approval (fig. 53).

FIG. 53. CATHOLIC CHURCH, Province of Lima, *Tercero cathecismo*.

PRAGMÁTICA
SOBRE LOS DIEZ DIAS DEL AÑO.

Don Philippe por la gracia de Dios, Rey de Castilla, de León, de Aragon, delas dos Sicilias, de Hierusalem, de Portogal, de Nauarra, de Granada, de Toledo, de Valencia, de Galicia, de Mallorca, de Seuilla, de Cerdeña, de Cordoua, de Corcega, de Murcia, de Iaen, delos Algarues, de Algezira, de Gibraltar, delas yslas de Canaria, de las Indias orientales, y occidentales, Yslas, y tierra firme, del mar Oceano, Archiduque de Austria, Duque de Borgoña, de Brauáte, y Milan, Conde de Habspurg, de Flandes, Tirol, y de Barcelona, señor de Bizcaya, y de Molina. &c.

Al Serenisimo Principe Don Philippe, mi muy caro, y muy amado hijo, y a los Infantes, Perlados, Duques, Marqueses, Códes, ricos hóbres, Maestres de las Ordenes, Priores, Comédadores, y Subcomédadores, Alcaydes delos Castillos, y Casas suertes, y llanas, y a los del nuestro Cósejo, Virreyes, Presidentes, y Oydores delas nuestras Audiécias Reales, Alcaldes, Gouernadores, Veyntey quatros, Caualleros, Escuderos, Officiales, y Hombres buenos, de todas las ciudades, villas, y lugares, delas nras Yndias, Yslas, y Tierra firme, del mar oceano, assi a los que agora son, como a los q adeláte fueré, y a cada vno, y qualquier de vos. Sabed, q nuestro muy sancto Padre Gregorio XIII. conformandose con la costumbre, y tradiction dela Yglesia catholica, y con lo dispuesto por el sacro Concilio Niceno, y con lo que vltimamente se desseo enel sancto Concilio de Trento, en razon de q las Pascuas, y otras fiestas se celebrassen a sus deuidos tiépos, ordeno vn Kalédario ecclesiastico, enel qual para enmendar, y reformar el yerro, q se auia ydo causando ẽla cuéta del curso del Sol, y dela Luna, se mandaron quitar diez dias del mes de Octubre del año passado de ochenta y dos (como se hizo) cótado quinze de octubre, quando se auiá de contar cinéo, y de ay adeláte, consecutiuamẽte hasta los treynta y vno, y q todos los otros meses del dicho año, y delos demas corriessen por la cuenta q hasta agora. Có lo qual, y cierta declaracion, q su Sanctidad haze, q du el dicho año, y quedan los venideros reformados: de suerte que las dichas Pascuas, y fiestas se vendrá a celebrar perpetuamente, a los tiempos que deué, y q los Padres sanctos antiguos, y q el sancto cócilio Niceno determinaron, segun q enel dicho Kalendario, y breue, q mando despachar su Sanctidad largamente se contiene. Y queriendome yo conformar en todo (como es razon) có lo q su Beatitud ha có tanto cuydado, y deliberacion ordenado, he mádado escriuir a los Arçobispos, y Obispos, y Prelados de essas partes, q hagan publicar el dicho Kalédario, y guardarle en todo, segú, y por la forma, q enel se cótiene este presente año de M. D. LXXXIII. Y por q si esta cuéta se vuiesse de guardar para solo celebrar las fiestas dela Yglesia, podria causar cófusion, y otras dubdas, en daño de mis subditos, y vassallos. Y para q esto cesse, queriendo proueer enello de remedio platicado enel mi Cósejo, y cómigo

FIG. 51. *Pragmática sobre los diez días del año.*

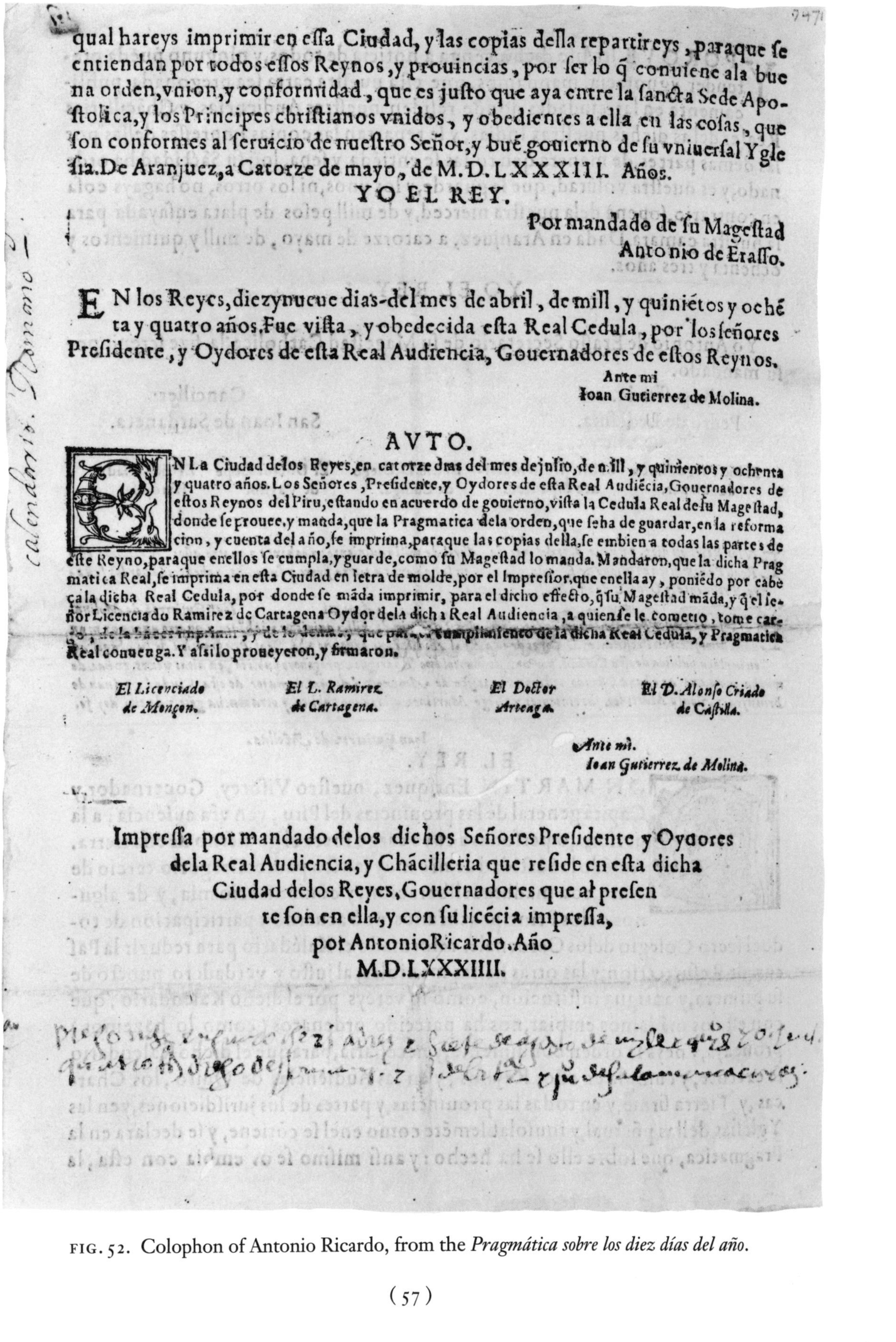

qual hareys imprimir en essa Ciudad, y las copias della repartireys, paraque se entiendan por todos essos Reynos, y prouincias, por ser lo q̃ conuiene ala buena orden, vnion, y conformidad, que es justo que aya entre la sancta Sede Apostolica, y los Principes christianos vnidos, y obedientes a ella en las cosas, que son conformes al seruicio de nuestro Señor, y bué gouierno de su vniuersal Yglesia. De Aranjuez, a Catorze de mayo, de M.D.LXXXIII. Años.

YO EL REY.

Por mandado de su Magestad
Antonio de Erasso.

E N los Reyes, diezynueue dias del mes de abril, de mill, y quiniétos y ochéta y quatro años. Fue vista, y obedecida esta Real Cedula, por los señores Presidente, y Oydores de esta Real Audiencia, Gouernadores de estos Reynos.

Ante mi
Ioan Gutierrez de Molina.

AVTO.

N La Ciudad de los Reyes, en catorze dias del mes de julio, de n.ill, y quinientos y ochenta y quatro años. Los Señores, Presidente, y Oydores de esta Real Audiécia, Gouernadores de estos Reynos del Piru, estando en acuerdo de gouierno, vista la Cedula Real de su Magestad, donde se prouee, y manda, que la Pragmatica dela orden, que seha de guardar, en la reformacion, y cuenta del año, se imprima, paraque las copias della, se embien a todas las partes de este Reyno, paraque en ellos se cumpla, y guarde, como su Magestad lo manda. Mandaron, que la dicha Pragmatica Real, se imprima en esta Ciudad en letra de molde, por el Impressor, que en ella ay, poniédo por cabeça la dicha Real Cedula, por donde se máda imprimir, para el dicho effecto, q̃ su Magestad máda, y q̃ el señor Licenciado Ramirez de Cartagena Oydor dela dich a Real Audiencia, a quien se le cometio, tome cargo, de la hazer imprimir, y de lo demas, que par cumplimiento de la dicha Real Cedula, y Pragmatica Real conuenga. Y assi lo proueyeron, y firmaron.

El Licenciado de Monçon.	El L. Ramirez de Cartagena.	El Doctor Arteaga.	El D. Alonso Criado de Castilla.

Ante mi.
Ioan Gutierrez de Molina.

Impressa por mandado delos dichos Señores Presidente y Oydores
dela Real Audiencia, y Chácilleria que reside en esta dicha
Ciudad delos Reyes, Gouernadores que al presen
te son en ella, y con su licécia impressa,
por Antonio Ricardo. Año
M.D.LXXXIIII.

FIG. 52. Colophon of Antonio Ricardo, from the *Pragmática sobre los diez días del año*.

The *Tercero cathecismo* was designed to instruct Indians who spoke two of the Peruvian viceroyalty's principal languages, Quechua and Aymara, both of which are widely used today. This particular edition, with its Spanish version of the catechism, continues to facilitate the study of both American tongues (fig. 54). Early Lima imprints such as this are exceedingly rare.

35.

Luis de Valdivia (1561–1642). *Doctrina christiana y cathecismo en la lengua allentiac*. Lima, 1607.

Lima's press was later used to produce works for the conversion of Indians who lived beyond the borders of the old Inca empire. The Jesuit Father, Luis de Valdivia, who specialized in the native languages of Chile and Argentina, translated this doctrinal work for these nomadic Indians and formulated vocabularies and grammars for the friars who instructed them. Unlike Quechua, which is still spoken by ten million South American Indians, Allentiac, the language of the inhabitants of the Argentine region of Cuyo, is now extinct. Only two copies of this work are known to be in the United States (fig. 55).

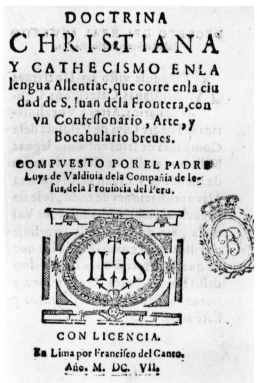

FIG. 55. Luis de Valdivia, *Doctrina christiana*.

36.

José de Acosta (1539–1616). *De natura Novi Orbis*. Cologne, 1596.

In addition to being a guiding force in the religious conversion of Peru's Indians, Father Acosta was a distinguished professor at Lima's University of San Marcos. His comprehensive history of the Indies, first published in Salamanca in 1588, deals with the

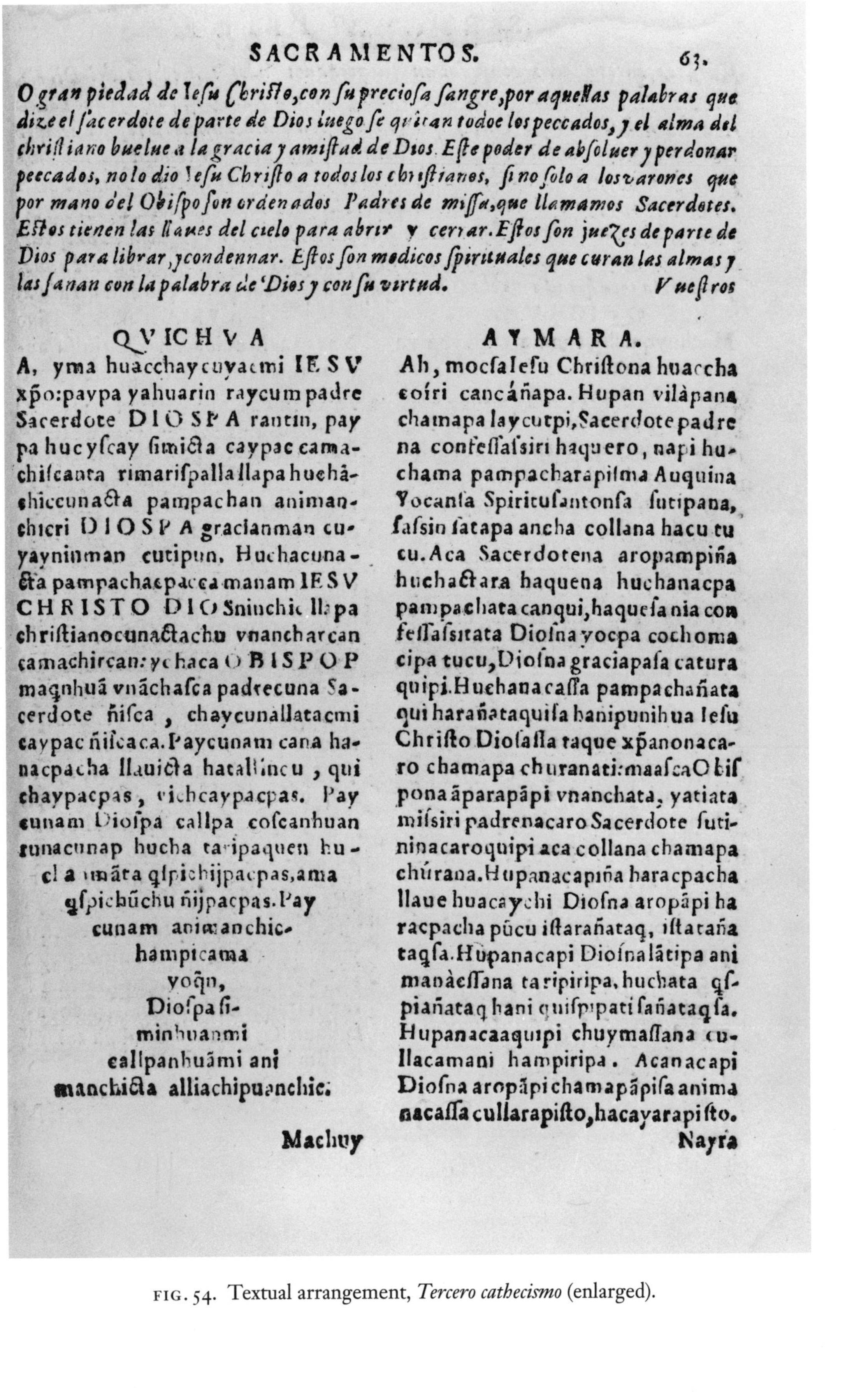

O gran piedad de Iesu Christo, con su preciosa sangre, por aquellas palabras que dize el sacerdote de parte de Dios iuego se quitan todoe los peccados, y el alma del christiano buelue a la gracia y amistad de Dios. Este poder de absoluer y perdonar peccados, no lo dio Iesu Christo a todos los christianos, sino solo a los varones que por mano del Obispo son ordenados Padres de missa, que llamamos Sacerdotes. Estos tienen las llaues del cielo para abrir y cerrar. Estos son iuezes de parte de Dios para librar, y condennar. Estos son medicos spirituales que curan las almas y las sanan con la palabra de Dios y con su virtud.

Vuestros

QVICHVA

A, yma huacchaycuyacmi IESV xpo:paupa yahuarin raycum padre Sacerdote DIOSPA rantin, pay pa hucyscay simicta caypac camachiscanta rimarispalla llapa hucháshiccunacta pampachan animanchicri DIOSPA gracianman cuyayninman cutipun. Huchacunacta pampachacpacca manam IESV CHRISTO DIOSninchic llapa christianocunactachu vnancharcan camachircan: ychaca OBISPOP magnhuã vnáchasca padrecuna Sacerdote ñisca, chaycunallatacmi caypac ñiscaca. Paycunam cana hanacpacha llauicta hatallíncu, qui chaypacpas, vichcaypacpas. Pay cunam Diospa callpa coscanhuan runacunap hucha taripaquen hucl a mata qispichijpacpas, ama qispichúchu ñijpacpas. Pay cunam animanchic hampicama yoqn, Diospa si minhuanmi callpanhuãmi ani manchicta alliachipuanchic.

Machuy

AYMARA.

Ah, mocsaIesu Christona huaccha coiri cancáñapa. Hupan vilápana chamapa laycutpi, Sacerdote padre na confessaisiri haquero, napi huchama pampacharapima Auquina Yocan[a Spiritu[antonsa sutipana, sassin satapa ancha collana hacu tu cu. Aca Sacerdotena aropampiña huchactara haquena huchanacpa pampachata canqui, haque[a nia con fessassitata Diosna yocpa cochoma cipa tucu, Diosna graciapasa catura quipi. Huchanacassa pampachañata qui harañataqui[a hanipunihua Iesu Christo Dios[asa taque xpanonacaro chamapa churanati: maasca Obis pona ãparapãpi vnanchata, yatiata missiri padrenacaro Sacerdote suti ninacaroquipi aca collana chamapa chúrana. Hupanacapiña haracpacha llaue huacaychi Diosna aropãpi ha racpacha pucu istarañataq, istaña taq[a. Hupanacapi Diosnalãtipa ani manàessana taripiripa, huchata qs piañataq hani quispipati[añataq[a. Hupanacaaquipi chuymassana cu llacamani hampiripa. Acanacapi Diosna aropãpi chamapãpi[a anima nacassa cullarapisto, hacayarapisto.

Nayra

FIG. 54. Textual arrangement, *Tercero cathecismo* (enlarged).

geography and natural history of the New World as well as the culture of its inhabitants. His detailed description of the customs of both North and South American Indians provides information about their religion, history, politics, and education, and he was one of the first historians to suggest that the native peoples of the Western Hemisphere came originally from Asia.

37.

PERU. *Ordencas* [sic] *que el señor marques de Cañete visorey de estos reynos del Piru mando hazer para el remedio de los excessos.* Ciudad de los Reyes [Lima], [1594].

Antonio Ricardo also printed a number of secular works, many of which deal with aspects of colonial administration. Among them is a set of ordinances approved by the Viceroy to stop the abuse of the natives by *corregidores*, or Indian agents. These minor officials played a critical role as liaison between the Spanish government and the Indian population, and they served as tax collectors, peace officers, and judges in indigenous communities. Unfortunately, many *corregidores* viewed the office as a means of enriching themselves, and they demanded both goods and services from their Indian charges. Creoles, Spaniards born in the New World, were especially upset by the *Ordenanças* because the office of *corregidor* was one of the few imperial appointments for which they were considered eligible. At this time, appointments to government positions were routinely granted only to peninsular-born Spaniards.

The *Ordenanças* in the John Carter Brown Library is the only recorded copy of this work in the United States.

38.

UNIVERSIDAD NACIONAL MAYOR DE SAN MARCOS. *Constituciones y ordenanças de la Universidad.* Ciudad de los Reyes [Lima], 1602.

In 1551, Charles I authorized the establishment of a system of royal and pontifical universities in Spanish America, which were modeled on the University of Salamanca. Although the University of San Marcos, the constitution and laws of which are printed here, claims that its charter was signed before that of Mexico, the latter institution opened its doors to students in 1553, and was therefore the first to offer courses.

Ricardo printed the rules and regulations governing San Marcos, and these documents contain a description of its organization, administration, faculty, and curriculum (fig. 56). Because they were considered to be the University's official policy, the constitution and ordinances were reprinted in Spain on several occasions. This is one of only two copies of this work recorded in the United States.

CONSTI
TVCIONES Y
ORDENANÇAS
DE LA VNIVERSIDAD, Y
STVDIO GENERAL DE LA
ciudad de los Reyes del Piru.

IMPRESSO EN LA-CIVDAD DE LOS
Reyes con licencia del señor Vísorey Don Luis
de Velasco, por Antonio Ricardo,
natural de Turin.

MDCII.

FIG. 56. *Constituciones y ordenanças de la Universidad* (San Marcos, Lima).

39.

ALONSO DE ERCILLA Y ZÚÑIGA (1533–1594). *La Araucana.* Madrid, 1590.

After the conquest of Peru, the Spaniards sought to extend the viceroyalty into northern Chile. Repeated incursions brought little immediate success against the area's nomadic Araucanian Indians, but the epic poem by the soldier Alonso de Ercilla immortalized the campaigns and extolled the courage and skills of warriors on both sides (fig. 57). The elegance and precision of the poem's royal octaves distinguish it among other Spanish epics, and the ideals it expresses are an aspect of Chilean national pride.

This is the first edition to incorporate all three parts of the work, the first part of which appeared in Madrid in 1569. Only three copies of the complete 1590 edition are known to be in the United States.

40.

PEDRO DE OÑA (1570? – 1643?). *Arauco domado.* Ciudad de los Reyes [Lima], 1596.

This epic poem written by Pedro de Oña, one of Chile's first poets, was commissioned by the family of Don García Hurtado de Mendoza in order to enhance his image as a military leader after he became Viceroy of Peru. As a young man, he led the campaigns against the Indians in Arauco, or Chile, but Alonso de Ercilla had failed to portray him as the hero of the expedition in his famous rhymed chronicle, *La Araucana.*

Arauco domado was praised for its extraordinary artistry by the Spanish master, Lope de Vega. Printed by Antonio Ricardo, it is the earliest book of poetry written by an American author and published in the New World. This volume contains a portrait of Oña (fig. 58), believed to be the first locally prepared illustration to appear in a South American book. The woodcut was probably executed by Ricardo or one of his assistants.

41.

PEDRO DE OÑA (1570? – 1643?). *Temblor de Lima año de 1609.* Lima, 1609.

The mountain ranges that extend through Mexico and Central America, and the Andes in South America, have been a constant source of seismic activity. Indian legends tell of the enormous destruction caused by earthquakes long before the arrival of the Spaniards, and they were the subject of colonial writing as well. An account of one that struck Guatemala City, published by Juan Pablos in 1541, was the earliest news report printed in the New World. In 1609, before newspapers had been established in Lima, Pedro de Oña wrote a poem describing the effects of a quake in that city (fig. 59).

Temblor de Lima was printed by Ricardo's successor, Francisco del Canto, who produced his first work in 1605. He is credited with the introduction of two-color

FIG. 57. Portrait of Ercilla, from ALONSO
DE ERCILLA Y ZÚÑIGA, *La Araucana*.

FIG. 58. Portrait of Oña, from PEDRO DE OÑA,
Arauco domado.

printing to the City of Kings, and it was under his imprint that books were published
at Julí, the remote Jesuit mission near Lake Titicaca. Although Canto was not directly
involved with the press in Julí, the name of his licensed publishing house on missionary
publications probably exempted them from close scrutiny by ecclesiastical censors.

This copy of *Temblor de Lima* is apparently unique in the United States.

42.

EL INCA GARCILASO DE LA VEGA (1539–1616). *Primera parte de los commentarios* [sic] *reales*. Lisbon, 1609.

Descriptions of Indian culture and the conquest of the Americas were not the exclusive
subjects of European historians and chroniclers. Accounts by Indians and mestizos such
as Don Fernando de Alva Ixtlilxochitl (1568–1648) in Mexico, and Felipe Guaman Poma
de Ayala (1526?–after 1613) and the Inca Garcilaso de la Vega in Peru, offer a new
perspective on the people and events of the time and portray more vividly the clash of
these different cultures.

FIG. 59. PEDRO DE OÑA, *Temblor de Lima.*   FIG. 60. EL INCA GARCILASO DE LA VEGA,
                                                    Comentarios reales.

In his *Comentarios reales*, the Inca Garcilaso de la Vega preserves the oral tradition
of a civilization that achieved greatness in many respects but failed to develop a form of
writing. As the son of an Inca princess and one of Pizarro's soldiers, he heard his
mother's relatives recount the myths and legends of their heritage, and he recorded
them in eloquent Spanish prose (fig. 60).

In Chapter xv of the first book of the *Comentarios reales*, the Inca tells the story of
the appearance of the first Incas and the founding of their empire. According to tradition,
Manco Capac and his sister-wife Mama Ocllo were sent to earth by the Sun to establish
their royal line. Leaving the shores of Lake Titicaca, they traveled in a northwesterly
direction. With them they carried a gold rod, which would enter the ground at the exact
location for the construction of their court, the future site of the city of Cuzco.

43.

MIGUEL SUÁREZ DE FIGUEROA. *Templo de N. grande patriarca San Francisco de
la provincia de los doce apostoles de el Peru.* Lima, 1675.

The Catholic Church in the Spanish American colonies left many monuments that are
indicative of its wealth and power in the New World. Among them is the convent church

of San Francisco in Lima, an excellent example of Humanistic architecture inspired by Italian design. This book by Suárez de Figueroa describes the structure's rededication in 1675 after earthquake damage had been repaired. It contains the only known colonial engraving in which the entire edifice is depicted (fig. 61).

44.

ALONSO CARRIÓ DE LA VANDERA (CONCOLORCORVO) (b. *c.*1706). *El lazarillo de ciegos caminantes desde Buenos-Ayres, hasta Lima*. Gijón [Lima], [1775 or 1776].

Inspired by the ideas of the Enlightenment, Charles III of Spain sought to reform the administration of the Spanish American colonies. In 1771, Alonso Carrió de la Vandera, who had been appointed by the Bourbon monarch, began his inspection tour of the South American postal system. After completing his journey, however, his recommendations for change were rejected by the bureaucracy. Disillusioned by this response, Carrió wrote a literary account of the episode, which is a general critique of Spanish American society and an excellent example of Menippean satire produced in the New World.

In order to protect himself from retaliation, Carrió presented the work as an account written by his Indian guide, Concolorcorvo, and gave a false date and place of publication for the book. The work, which was probably unlicensed, was printed in Lima in 1775 or 1776 and not in Spain as stated on the title page (fig. 62). The publishing house "La Rovada" translates as "Something Stolen."

45.

Mercurio Peruano de historia, literatura, y noticias públicas. Lima, [1791] – 1795.

The circulation of news in printed form probably began in South America in 1594. At that time Antonio Ricardo published a fifteen-page pamphlet on the English pirate Richard Hawkins, who had been sent by Sir Francis Drake to disrupt Spanish trade and commerce along the South American coast. News was distributed on a regular basis throughout most of the seventeenth century, and in 1744 the first Peruvian newspaper, *La Gaceta de Lima*, was established. It was followed by the *Mercurio Peruano*, an exceptional periodical published by the "Sociedad Económica de Amantes del País" (fig. 63). Influenced by the Enlightenment, members of this organization expressed an interest in everything from literary trends to political change, and they stood at the forefront of Peru's intellectual life. Although the *Mercurio Peruano* disseminated much information, such as the results of a 1790 census of Lima (fig. 64), government pressure forced it to cease publication after only five years.

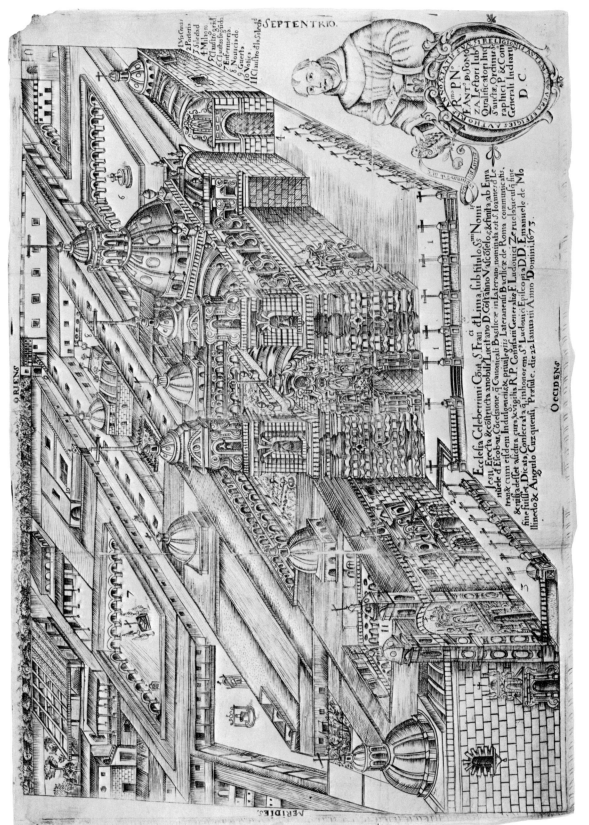

FIG. 61. The Convent Church of San Francisco, from MIGUEL SUÁREZ DE FIGUEROA, *Templo de N. Grande Patriarca San Francisco* (Lima).

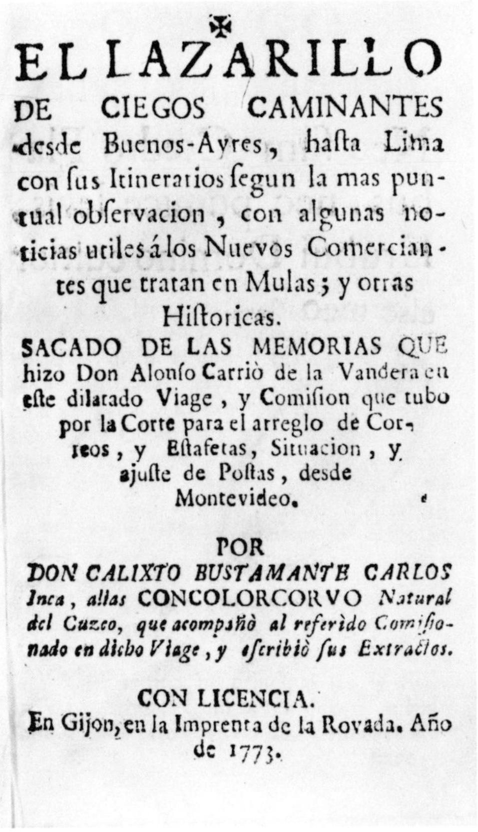

EL LAZARILLO
DE CIEGOS CAMINANTES
desde Buenos-Ayres, hasta Lima
con sus Itinerarios segun la mas puntual observacion, con algunas noticias utiles á los Nuevos Comerciantes que tratan en Mulas; y otras
Historicas.
SACADO DE LAS MEMORIAS QUE
hizo Don Alonso Carrió de la Vandera en
este dilatado Viage, y Comision que tubo
por la Corte para el arreglo de Correos, y Estafetas, Situacion, y
ajuste de Postas, desde
Montevideo.

POR
DON CALIXTO BUSTAMANTE CARLOS
Inca, alias CONCOLORCORVO Natural
del Cuzco, que acompañò al referido Comisionado en dicho Viage, y escribiò sus Extractos.

CON LICENCIA.
En Gijon, en la Imprenta de la Rovada. Año
de 1773.

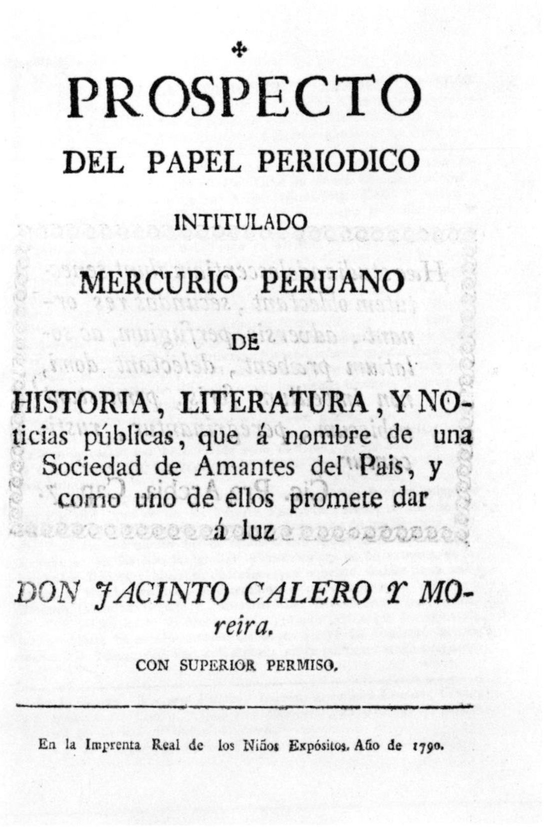

PROSPECTO
DEL PAPEL PERIODICO
INTITULADO
MERCURIO PERUANO
DE
HISTORIA, LITERATURA, Y NO-
ticias públicas, que á nombre de una
Sociedad de Amantes del Pais, y
como uno de ellos promete dar
á luz

DON JACINTO CALERO Y MO-
reira.

CON SUPERIOR PERMISO.

En la Imprenta Real de los Niños Expósitos. Año de 1790.

FIG.62. ALONSO CARRIÓ DE LA VAN-
DERA, *El lazarillo de ciegos caminantes.*

FIG.63. *Mercurio Peruano* (Lima).

THE CAPTAINCY-GENERAL OF CHILE

46.

El Monitor Araucano. Santiago, 1813–1814.

By the middle of the eighteenth century, through the efforts of the German Jesuit Carlos Haimhausen, the printing press had arrived in Chile. The expulsion of the Society of Jesus from Spanish domains in 1767, however, disrupted its operation and made the role of printing in Chilean life uncertain for many years.

The growth of the Chilean nationalist movement, however, increased the need for printed pamphlets and broadsides, and the equipment and artisans sent from the United States helped to re-establish printing. In 1812 the *Aurora de Chile,* the region's first newspaper, was founded, and the next year it was followed by *El Monitor Araucano* (fig.

Ciudad de LIMA, con distincion de clases y Estados,
Exc.mo Sr. Frey Don Francisco Gil Taboada y Lemos:

COMUNIDADES RELIGIOSAS.

MONGES.	Casas	Hospicios	Profesos.	Novicios.	Legos.	Donados.	Niños.	Criados.	Esclavos.	Total
Benitos	....	1	2	...	....	1	....	6	3	12
Gerónimos	....	1	1	...	....	....	....	2	....	3
MENDICANTES.										
Dominicos	4	....	161	7	36	29	1	11	27	272
Franciscanos	2	...	139	6	36	47	..	1	13	243
Descalzos	1	...	20	3	10	16	..	1	10	60
Missioneros de Ocopa	..	1	2	..	..	1	..	..	1	4
Agustinos	3	...	135	8	25	9	..	24	26	227
Mercedarios	3	...	146	12	27	6	5	10	22	228
Minimos	1	...	32	5	5	9	..	13	..	64
De S. Juan de Dios	1	...	7	6	30	3	..	3	4	53
Bethlemitas	2	...	3	5	22	12	..	..	3	45
Clerigos Reglares.										
Agonizantes	2	....	36	....	22	13	....	1	16	88
CONGREGACIONES										
De S. Felipe Neri	1	....	27	...	14	7	..	22	24	91
TOTALES	20	3	711	52	228	152	6	94	149	1.392

MONJAS.	Casas suget. al Ord.	Profesas.	Novicias.	Donadas.	Sras. Segl.s Seglares.	de Castas	Criadas.	Esclavas.	Donados.	Criados.	TOTAL
Bernardas	1	26	3	9	34	39	28	17	..	1	157
Dominicas	2	61	8	11	21	48	43	33	..	..	225
Franciscas Claras	1	38	7	24	30	60	50	34	..	1	244
Capuchinas	1	34	...	....	....	....	....	3	2	039
Concebidas	1	59	1	28	31	90	..	51	..	..	260
Idem Descalzas	1	24	3	12	21	30	20	45	..	..	155
Agustinas	2	69	7	21	31	63	46	30	..	1	268
Carmelitas Descalzas	2	41	..	..	..	36	1	5	5	088
Id. Nazaren. Descalz.	1	31	..	..	..	16	..	..	..	047
Trinitarias Descalzas	1	29	2	..	..	20	..	1	1	053
Mercedarias Descalz.	1	22	2	..	2	17	4	..	2	049
TOTALES	14	434	33	105	170	330	276	215	9	13	1585

BEATERIOS.	Casas.	Profesas.	Sras. Seglares.	Seglares de Castas.	Deposita das.	Criadas.	Esclavas.	Donadas.	Total.
Dominicas	1	16	16	..	..	19	2	..	53
Franciscas	1	24	16	..	..	17	5	1	63
Idem de Indias	1	18	2	21	..	5	..	..	47
Amparadas y Recog.	1	26	55	40	24	..	2	..	147
TOTALES	4	84	89	61	24	41	9	2	310

NOTA.

La distincion de Destinos y Categorías, no lleva suma particular, por que el objeto de esta division no es el de reasumir el numero total de Habitantes, sino se dirige á designar la clase de ocupaciones, y recursos que mas conocidamente influyen en la substentacion de los Vecinos de esta Capital.

Lima, y Diciembre 5. de 1790.

Joseph Maria de Egaña.

POBLACION COMPREHENDIDA EN EL RECINTO DE LA

instruido sobre los Datos de la enumeracion total de sus Individuos, mandada executar por el
Virrey de estos Reynos, baxo la direccion del Teniente de Policía Don Joseph María de Egaña.

ESTADO SECULAR.

CALIDADES.	SOLTEROS. Hombres.	Mugeres.	CASADOS. Hombres.	Mugeres.	VIUDOS. Hombres.	Mugeres.	TOTAL
Españoles	5225	4835	2740	2603	370	1442	17215
Indios	1426	929	684	631	80	162	3912
Mestizos	1357	1362	737	767	74	334	4631
Negros	3138	2737	1200	1250	153	482	8960
Mulatos	1831	2148	775	735	78	405	5972
Quarterones	728	815	345	290	43	162	2383
Quinterones	76	91	17	16	6	13	219
Zambos	1139	1308	312	349	102	174	3384
Chinos	385	414	135	117	26	43	1120
TOTALES	15.305	14639	6945	6758	932	3217	47796

TOTAL de Estados. | 29.944 | 13.703 | 4.149

TOTAL GENERAL .... § 47.796. §

POBLACION DE CADA QUARTEL.

QUARTEL 1	4661	4548	2458	2350	240	1049	15.306
QUARTEL 2	3831	3250	1461	1381	162	690	10.775
QUARTEL 3	4173	4020	1786	1794	261	732	12.766
QUARTEL 4	2640	2821	1232	1241	269	746	8.949
TOTALES	15305	14639	6937	6766	932	3217	47.796

TOTAL de Estados. | 29.944 | 13.703 | 4.149

DESTINOS, Y CATEGORIAS.

Curas . . . . . . 10.	Titulos . . . . . . 49.	Empl. con sueldo Rl. 426.
Tenientes de Cura. 19.	Hacendados . . . 90.	Con fuero Militar. 27.
Clerigos . . . . . 229.	Abogados . . . . . 91.	Empleados en Oficinas particulares 64.
Ordenad. de Menor. 16.	Escribanos . . . . 58.	
Sachristanes . . . 34.	Comerciantes , . 393.	Sindicos de Religion. 10.
Notarios . . . . . 13.	Fábricantes . . . 60.	Medicos . . . . . 21.
Depend. de Inquisi. 15.	Artesanos . . . 1027.	Cirujanos . . . . 56.
Idem de Cruzada ..06.	Labradores . . . 308.	Abastecedores ..48.
Estudiantes . . . 366.	Jornaleros . . . 363.	Cobrad. de Cofrad. 47.
Demandantes . . . 52.	Sirvientes blancos. 474.	Pulperos . . . . . 287.

Sirvient. de Cast. libres.
Hombres . . . . 1284.
Mugeres . . . . 1619. } ... 2903.

Esclavos.
Hombres. 5063.
Mugeres...4166. } ...9229.

RESUMEN GENERAL:

Existentes por el Estado Secular de todas clases	Hombres	23.182	47.796
	Mugeres	24.614	
Por el total de Religiosos Profesos	Hombres	991	1.647
	Mugeres	656	
Vivientes en Comunidades sin Votos	Hombres	1.564	3.184
	Mugeres	1.620	
Total de la Poblacion de esta Capital	Hombres	25.737	52.627
	Mugeres	26.890	

NOTA. En el total de la Poblacion,
no están inclusos los sugetos á revista.

COMUNIDADES CIVILES.

COLEGIOS.	Rectores.	Maestros.	Pensionarios.	Pensionistas.	Criados.	Esclavos.	TOTAL.
Real de S. Carlos.	1	15	55	17	11	10	109
Santo Toribio.	1	19	23	29	9	4	85
El Princ. de Caciques	1	02	05	05	4		17
TOTALES	3	30	83	51	24	14	211

Idem de Mugeres.	Rectoras.	Maestras.	Pensionistas.	Pensionarias.	Criadas.	Esclavas.	TOTAL.
La Caridad.	1		18	6	7	5	37
Sta. Cruz de Huerfanas.	1	2	24		2		20
TOTALES	2	2	42	6	9	5	66

HOSPITALES.	Capellanes	Empleados. Hombres.	Muger. res.	Facultativ.	Sirvientes. Hombres.	Muge res.	Enfermos Hombres.	Muge res.	Locos Hombres.	Muge res.	Esclavos.	Total.
S. Pedro de Clerigos.				1	2		5					19
San Andres de Españ.	4	7		8	24		166		49		6	264
Espir. Sto. de Mariner.	2	3		4	7		35				2	53
San Juan de Dios, de Convalecientes.							5				2	7
Bethlemitas de Idem.							20	3			3	27
Incurables.							9	7				17
San Lázaro.	2	2					16	9				29
La Carid. de Españ.	3	3	3	3	1	14	74		6	16		123
Camilas.			10			5			4			24
Sta. Ana de Indios.	4	12	3	6	16	7	108	29		15		200
S. Bartolomé de Neg.	3	5		4	5	2	86	68		5	5	184
TOTALES	18	32	19	26	55	28	456	195	54	11	53	947

Casas de Misericord.	Empleados.	Sirvientes.	Expósitos.	Expósitas.	Hombres.	Mugeres.	Total.
Inclusa	4	3	27	20			54
Hospicio	1				29		31
Casa de Mug. pobres						53	54
TOTALES	6	3	27	20	29	54	139

CARCELES.	Españoles. Hombres.	Mugeres.	De Castas. Hombres.	Mugeres.	Empleados.	Total.
De Corte	29		70	4	3	106
De la Ciudad	9		57	5	3	74
De Inquisicion					1	1
TOTALES	38		127	9	7	181

NOTA.

La Subdivision, y numero de Sirvientes libres, y esclavos, no es una nueva agregacion á los Estados Religioso, Secular, y de Comunidades Civiles; si no una parte de ellos, inclusa ya en sus respectivos totales, y distinguida luego para mayor ilustracion del Estado general, y como por Apéndice á la casilla particular de distinciones de Destinos, y Categorías.

Dado á luz por la Sociedad Académica de Amantes del Pais, Autora del *Mercurio Peruano*.

Impreso en la Imprenta Real de Niños Expósitos.

FIG. 64. The 1790 census of Lima, from *Mercurio Peruano*.

65). Both periodicals were used to circulate news about the latest developments in the campaign for independence and to increase patriotic fervor among Chile's residents.

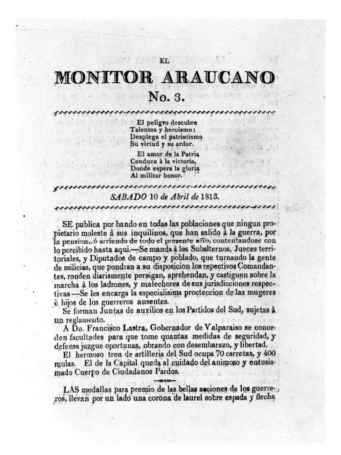

FIG. 65. *El Monitor Araucano* (Santiago de Chile).

47.

JOSÉ DE SAN MARTÍN (1778–1850). *Proclama a los habitantes del estado de Chile.* [Santiago, 1820].

In 1817 the liberator José de San Martín crossed the Andes into Chile, a journey that took men, livestock, and military machinery through mountain passes more than two miles above sea level. After winning battles at Chacabuco and Maipú, San Martín made lengthy preparations for the next and most crucial phase of his campaign, the march northward and the assault on royalist troops in Peru. This 1820 broadside (fig. 66), issued four years before the last battle for independence from Spain, is an open declaration of rebellion and calls on all Americans to preserve civil order while the armies readied themselves for the coming campaign against the royalists.

1824 (Junio 17)

PROCLAMA
A LOS HABITANTES
del Estado de Chile.

---*---

COMPATRIOTAS:

Al fin se acerca el dia tan suspirado por vosotros, como por nuestros hermanos del Perú. El Supremo Director y el Excmo. Senado, de acuerdo con el sufragio universal de Chile, me han encargado la direccion de la grande empresa, cuyo resultado aguarda el mundo, para declararnos por rebeldes, si somos vencidos, ó reconocer nuestros derechos, si triunfamos.— Voy á cumplir sus designios, y responder de la confianza que se me há hecho, con la victoria ó con la muerte.

Pero antes de separarme de vosotros, permitidme que os encarezca la necesidad de conservar el órden: la experiencia os ha enseñado á conocer sus ventajas; y las calamidades que sufren los pueblos, que han caido en la anarquía, deben hacer temblar á los que no aprecien el sosiego. El Gobierno que os rige, no és, ni puede ser tan perfecto, como sus propios intereses y los vuestros exigen que lo sea: mas sus intenciones son justas y equitativas: ellas no tienen otro objeto que el bien público, y si alguna vez no alcanza su acierto hasta donde se extiende su zelo, acordaos de las circunstancias en que nos hallamos, del gobierno Español bajo cuya influencia hemos vivido, y del tiempo que hace que tomamos las armas contra su injusticia.

Compatriotas! Voy á abrir la campaña mas memorable de nuestra revolucion: de ella penden, la consolidacion de nuestros destinos, las esperanzas de este vasto continente, la suerte de nuestras familias, la fortuna de nuestros amigos, en fin, lo mas sagrado, que es nuestro honor. Fiado en la justicia de nuestra causa, y en la proteccion del Ser Supremo, yo os prometo la victoria, y no dudo que ella coronará como hasta aqui la constancia de los valientes que me acompañan.

Cuartel general en Santiago Junio 17 de 1820.

San Martin

FIG. 66. JOSÉ DE SAN MARTÍN, *Proclama a los habitantes del Estado de Chile.*

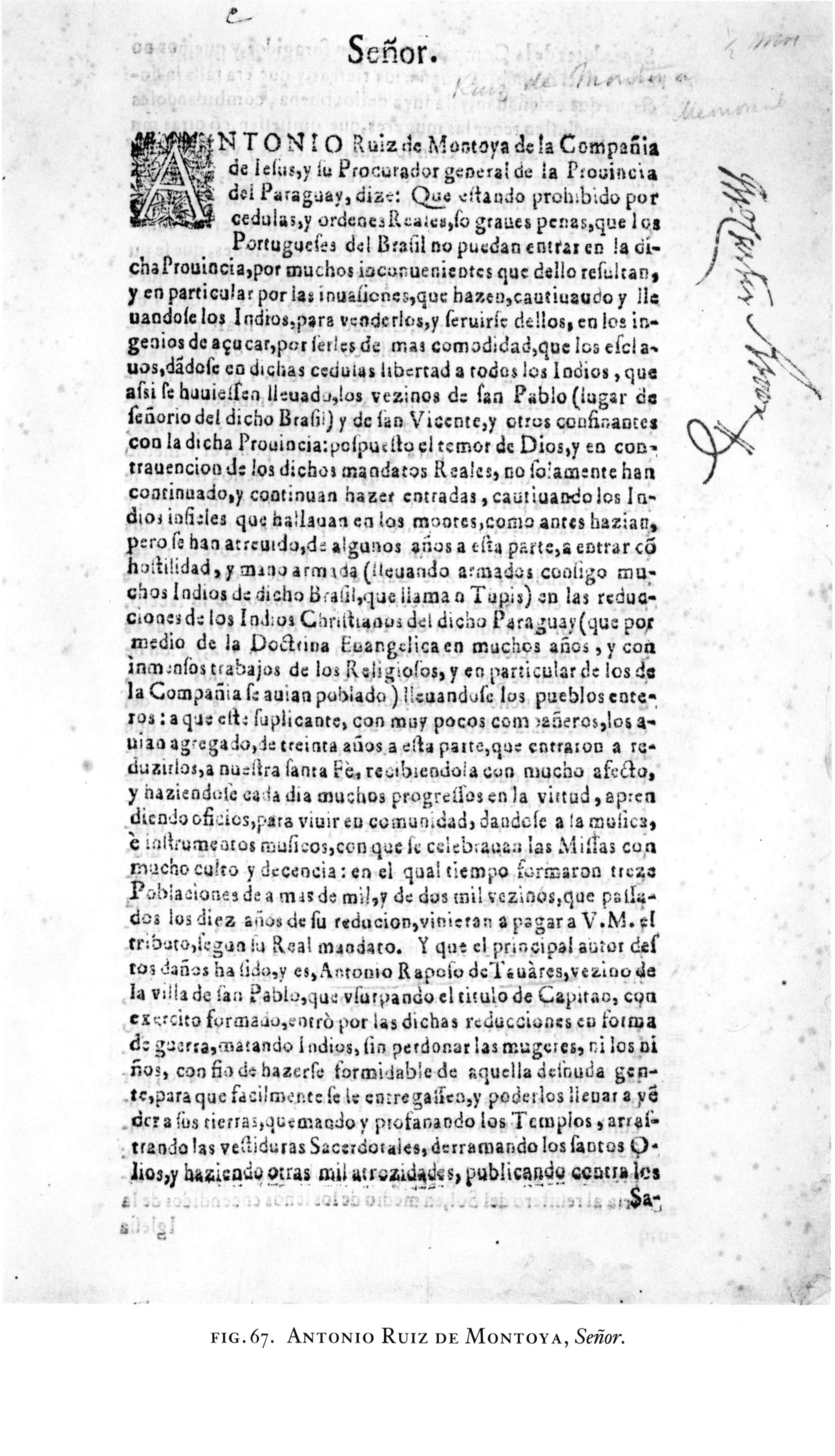

Señor.

ANTONIO Ruiz de Montoya de la Compañia de Iesus, y su Procurador general de la Prouincia del Paraguay, dize: Que estando prohibido por cedulas, y ordenes Reales, so graues penas, que los Portugueses del Brasil no puedan entrar en la dicha Prouincia, por muchos inconuenientes que dello resultan, y en particular por las inuasiones, que hazen, cautiuando y lleuandose los Indios, para venderlos, y seruirse dellos, en los ingenios de açucar, por serles de mas comodidad, que los esclauos, dádose en dichas cedulas libertad a todos los Indios, que assi se huuiessen lleuado, los vezinos de san Pablo (lugar de señorio del dicho Brasil) y de san Vicente, y otros confinantes con la dicha Prouincia: pospuesto el temor de Dios, y en contrauencion de los dichos mandatos Reales, no solamente han continuado, y continuan hazer entradas, cautiuando los Indios infieles que hallauan en los montes, como antes hazian, pero se han atreuido, de algunos años a esta parte, a entrar có hostilidad, y mano armada (lleuando armados consigo muchos Indios de dicho Brasil, que llaman Tupis) en las reducciones de los Indios Christianos del dicho Paraguay (que por medio de la Doctrina Euangelica en muchos años, y con inmensos trabajos de los Religiosos, y en particular de los de la Compañia se auian poblado) lleuandose los pueblos enteros: a que este suplicante, con muy pocos compañeros, los auian agregado, de treinta años a esta parte, que entraron a reduzirlos, a nuestra santa Fè, recibiendola con mucho afecto, y haziendose cada dia muchos progressos en la virtud, aprendiendo oficios, para viuir en comunidad, dandose a la musica, e instrumentos musicos, con que se celebrauan las Missas con mucho culto y decencia: en el qual tiempo formaron treze Poblaciones de a mas de mil, y de dos mil vezinos, que passados los diez años de su reducion, vinieran a pagar a V.M. el tributo, segun su Real mandato. Y que el principal autor destos daños ha sido, y es, Antonio Raposo de Teuàres, vezino de la villa de san Pablo, que vsurpando el titulo de Capitao, con exercito formado, entrò por las dichas reducciones en forma de guerra, matando Indios, sin perdonar las mugeres, ni los niños, con fin de hazerse formidable de aquella desnuda gente, para que facilmente se le entregassen, y poderlos lleuar a yéder a sus tierras, quemando y profanando los Templos, arrastrando las vestiduras Sacerdotales, derramando los santos Olios, y haziendo otras mil atrozidades, publicando contra los

Sa-

FIG. 67. Antonio Ruiz de Montoya, *Señor.*

The Viceroyalty of Río de la Plata

THE INTENDENCY OF PARAGUAY

48.

ANTONIO RUIZ DE MONTOYA (1585–1652). *Señor.* [Madrid, 1639 or 1640].

In 1537, after the outpost at Buenos Aires was destroyed by the Indians, the Spaniards made their way a thousand miles up the Paraguay River to build the area's first permanent settlement at Asunción. Half a century later, Jesuit missionaries began to enter Paraguay, which then included modern-day Uruguay, northern Argentina, and southern Brazil. The story of their successful establishment of *reducciones* or communal villages among the Guaraní Indians is the most dramatic in the history of Christian evangelism in the New World. The protection of their new converts, however, became a major concern for the Jesuits as Brazilian slave hunters from São Paulo continued to raid their settlements. In *Señor,* a letter of protest to the King of Spain, Father Antonio Ruiz de Montoya accused one Antonio Raposo de Tavares of having led a force from Buenos Aires in an attack on a Jesuit mission in Paraguay (fig. 67). This is the only recorded copy of the work in the United States.

49.

ANTONIO RUIZ DE MONTOYA (1585–1652). *Catecismo de la lengua guarani.* Madrid, 1640.

50.

ANTONIO RUIZ DE MONTOYA (1585–1652). *Arte, y bocabulario de la lengua guarani.* Madrid, 1640.

Father Antonio Ruiz de Montoya was not only a leader of the Jesuit *reducciones,* he was also a specialist in Guaraní linguistics. The catechism (fig. 68) and grammar (fig. 69), two of his early works, are among the first books ever printed in that South American language. Because there was no printing press in Paraguay, the Jesuits sent their manu-

26 *Doctrina Christiana.*

Mboraĩhú.
7. Ymo siete hába.
Yñãteỹrupiâ;
Quỹ reỹ.

Contra embidia.
7. La septima,
Diligencia
Contra pereza.

Los Enemigos del Anima.

ñande ãngĩ amota-
reỹhara:
Mbohapĩ.
1. Yỹipĩ, añãnga.

2. Ymõmõcõí hába,
Mbaeaí ĩbĩ peguá-
ra.
3. Ymõmboapĩ há-
ba,
Açé roó.

Los Enemigos del
anima,
Son tres.
1. El primero, el De
monio.
2. El segúdo, el Mú-
do.

3. El tercero, la Car
ne.

Las Virtudes Teologales.

Tecómãrãngatú
Tũ-

Las Virtudes
Que

en lengua Guaraní, y Castellana. 27

Tũpãrehéñãndemõ
. maê hába
Mbohapĩ nãngã.
1. Yỹipĩ Tũpãre-
robiâ.
2. Ymõmõcõí hába
Tũpãrehé yerobiâ.
3. Ymõmboapĩ há-
ba
Mboraĩhú.

Que llamamos
Teologales,
Son tres.
1. La primera,
Fè.
2. La segunda,
Esperança.
3. La tercera,

Caridad.

Cardinales.

Tecómãrãngatu ĩ
gué
Irũdĩ nãngá.
1. Yỹipĩ Tecó re-
nõndeá hába.
2. Ymõmocoí hába
Tecoyoyâ.
3. Ymõmboapĩhába
Açé ãng pĩ atã.
4. Ymõ irũdĩ hába
Mbaepabêrehe
Açé yeaĩnûbá.

Las Virtudes
Cardinales,
Son quatro.
1. La primera,
Prudencia.
2. La segunda,
Iusticia.
3. La tercera,
Fortaleza.
4. La quarta,
Templança.

Po-

FIG. 68. A page from ANTONIO RUIZ DE MONTOYA, *Catecismo.*

scripts to Spain, but they expressed concern over the ability of Spanish printers to set type accurately using the Guaraní alphabet that they had devised.

The acquisition of language skills played an important role in the organization and progress of the missions, forging a model for the development of Indian culture. Although the law stipulated that American natives were to be taught Spanish, it was not enforced at the time the Jesuits began establishing their missions in Paraguay. Thus they trained their Indian charges to read and write in their own language and standardized its usage through instruction. Critics of the Jesuits charged that they were creating an autonomous state within the Spanish American colonies whose citizens were being taught to resist Hispanization.

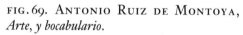

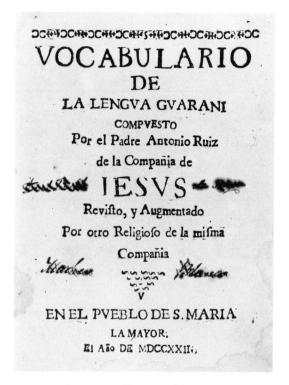

FIG. 69. ANTONIO RUIZ DE MONTOYA, *Arte, y bocabulario.*

FIG. 70. ANTONIO RUIZ DE MONTOYA, *Vocabulario de la lengua guaraní.*

51.

ANTONIO RUIZ DE MONTOYA (1585–1652). *Vocabulario de la lengua guarani.* Santa María la Mayor, 1722.

52.

ANTONIO RUIZ DE MONTOYA (1585–1652). *Arte de la lengua guarani.* Santa María la Mayor, 1724.

Although the Jesuits asked the crown for permission to establish a press soon after their arrival in Paraguay, years passed before it became a reality. Libraries did exist, however, and contained books sent from Spain, copies of works made by Indian scribes, and short pieces allegedly produced locally on a block press. Father Juan Baptista Neumann (1659–1705) built the earliest letterpress used in Paraguay and created the type needed for its operation. Native materials and labor were utilized as much as possible in all phases of the printing process, and only paper was imported from Spain. Among the titles printed between 1700 and 1727 were works by Father Montoya that had originally been published in Spain. Appearing some seventy years after Father Montoya's death, these extremely rare books (figs. 70 and 71) were excerpted from the *Arte y bocabulario* (1640).

Futuro.

Amboène) le enfeñare (erembo̊è) le enfeñarás &c.

Fut. Perfecto.

Amboe ĭmane) yá le avre enfeñado (eremboe ĭmane) yá
le avras enfeñado. &c.

Fut. y Pret. Mixto.

Amboe amobiñã) le avia de aver enfeñado, ynole en-
feñe (eremboè amobiñã) le avias de aver enfeñado &c.

Imperativo.

Emboe l. teremboe)   enfeñale tu.
Tomboè)   enfeñele aquel.
Pemboè l. tapemboe)   enfeñad le vofotros.
Tomboè)   enfeñen le aquellos.

Del verbo Ahaĭhu.

Ehaĭhu l. terehaĭhu)   amale tu.
Tohaĭhu   amale aquel.

Plural.

Pehaĭhu l. tapehaĭhú)   amad le vofotros.
Tohaĭhu)   aman le aquellos.

Nota.

Del Imperativo Prohibitivo.

El Prefente del Indicativo con la particula (teỹ)
y con (ne) prohibe, por efso lo llaman ̓mperativo
Prohibitivo, en la realidad es tiempo futuro, fe ufa de
efta manera (erehoteỹne) no vayas, (Peyapo teỹne)
nolo

FIG. 71. A page from ANTONIO RUIZ DE MONTOYA, *Arte de la lengua guaraní* (enlarged).

53.

ANTONIO GARRIGA (1662–1733). *Instruccion practica para ordenar santamente la vidà*. Loreto, 1713.

The first printing press in Paraguay was probably established in Loreto. It is unclear, however, whether it moved from place to place or whether other presses were actually built in the missionary stations of Santa María la Mayor, San Francisco Xavier, and possibly Candelaria. Remnants of an early press, which are housed today in the Museum of the Cabildo in Buenos Aires, were recovered from this general area and allegedly belonged to the Jesuit printing network. *Instrucción práctica*, a product of the Loreto press, is a guidebook for priests written by the Mallorcan Father, Antonio Garriga, who composed it in Chuquisaca on his trip from Lima to Córdoba (fig. 72). This is the only recorded copy of this book in the United States.

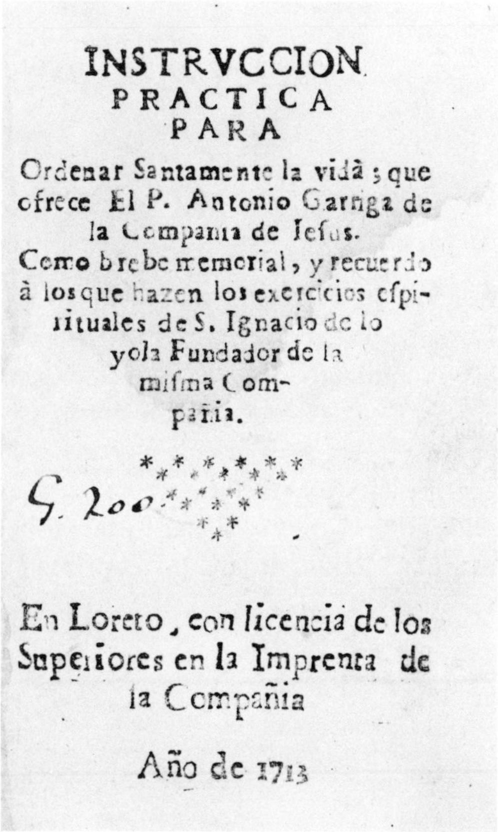

INSTRVCCION
PRACTICA
PARA
Ordenar Santamente la vidà; que
ofrece El P. Antonio Garriga de
la Compania de Iesus.
Como breve memorial, y recuerdo
à losque hazen los exercicios espirituales de S. Ignacio de lo
yola Fundador de la
misma Com-
pañia.

En Loreto, con licencia de los
Superiores en la Imprenta de
la Compañia
Año de 1713

FIG. 72. ANTONIO GARRIGA, *Instrucción práctica*.

54.

NICOLÁS YAPUGUAY. *Sermones y exemplos en lengua guarani*. Pueblo de San Francisco Xavier, 1727.

This collection of Guaraní sermons, written by Nicolás Yapuguay, was one of the last works to be printed in the Jesuits' communal villages. By the middle of the eighteenth century, there were about thirty missions in existence with approximately 100,000 Indians under their jurisdiction. The system flourished until 1767, when members of the Society of Jesus were expelled from Spanish America. Although the Indians may be said to have benefited from the Jesuits' paternalistic rule, they had not been taught how to manage the communities on their own. Despite the arrival of able replacements from other religious orders to supervise the Paraguayan missions, they soon disintegrated.

In 1753 José Quiroga (1707–1784), a member of the Society of Jesus in Paraguay, prepared a map of the Jesuit missions (fig. 73). The map, measuring 38″ by 31¾″, was engraved by Ferdinand Franceschelli and published in Rome.

THE INTENDENCY OF BUENOS AIRES

55.

JOSÉ ANTONIO DE SAN ALBERTO (1727–1804). *Carta circular, ó edicto*. Buenos Aires, 1781.

In 1764 the German Jesuit, Pablo Karrer, established a European printing press in Córdoba. When the Society of Jesus was expelled from the colonies three years later, however, all publication ceased, and the equipment from the print shop was confiscated. The Franciscans took over the university where the press was housed and, on the orders of the Viceroy Juan José de Vértiz y Salcedo, sent it to Buenos Aires in 1780. There it became known as the "Imprenta de los Niños Expósitos."

The *Carta circular*, issued by the Bishop of Córdoba del Tucumán, concerns advancement in religious orders. It was printed during the press's second year of operation.

FIG. 73. JOSÉ QUIROGA, *Mapa de las missiones.*

¶La relacion que dio Aluar nu=
ñez cabeça de vaca de lo acaescido enlas Indias
enla armada donde yua por gouernador Pã
philo de narbaez desde el año de veynte
y siete hasta el año ő treynta y seys
que boluio a Seuilla con tres
de su compañia.:.

FIG. 74. ALVAR NÚÑEZ CABEZA DE VACA, *La relación* (enlarged).

The North American Borderlands

56.

Alvar Núñez Cabeza de Vaca (1490? – 1559?). *La relacion de . . . lo acaescido en las Indias.* [Zamora, 1542].

Although no colonial presses were established in the Spanish territories that are now part of the southern United States, the region was of considerable interest to explorers, writers, scholars, and members of religious communities. The earliest account of a trip through this area was written by Alvar Núñez Cabeza de Vaca, who was treasurer of the ill-fated expedition sent to Florida in 1527. This unfortunate group of men was shipwrecked at the present site of Matagorda Bay, Texas, and Cabeza de Vaca and three other survivors spent nine years wandering in the wilderness before making their way to Sinaloa. His journal provides valuable ethnographic information about numerous native American tribes—and the profile of a Spaniard who found himself constantly at the mercy of the Indians (fig. 74).

57.

Fidalgo Delvas *or* "Gentleman of Elvas." *Relaçam verdadeira dos trabalhos q[ue] ho governador do[m] Ferna[n]do d[e] Souto [e] certos fidalgos portugueses passarom.* Evora, 1557.

This account by an anonymous Portuguese volunteer who accompanied Hernando de Soto on his expedition through the present southeastern United States contains the first description of the exploration of the Mississippi River and its delta (fig. 75). As a military mission, the expedition was deemed a failure because it did not uncover any wealthy civilizations and because De Soto died before its completion. The information gathered by the "Gentleman" from 1539 to 1543, however, enabled cartographers to determine correctly the shape of the land mass from Florida to the Mississippi River. This, together with facts provided by Cabeza de Vaca, led to the creation of maps of the entire southern part of the present United States drawn with considerable accuracy. Only two copies of this book are reported in the United States.

FIG. 75. "Gentleman of Elvas," *Rela-çam verdadeira*.

FIG. 76. El Inca Garcilaso de la Vega, *La florida*.

58.

El Inca Garcilaso de la Vega (1539–1616). *La Florida del Ynca. Historia del adelantado Hernando de Soto*. Lisbon, 1605.

Several other participants in De Soto's expedition returned to Spain at its conclusion, and there they met the Inca Garcilaso de la Vega, who had left his native Peru and was living near Córdoba. Making use of their detailed testimony, the Inca imaginatively reconstructed the important events of their daring march to the Mississippi (fig. 76). Such an account, he hoped, would stimulate interest in the area and encourage the Spanish to conquer and colonize it.

59.

Carlos de Sigüenza y Góngora (1645–1700). *Descripcion, que de la vaia de Santa Maria de Galve (antes Pansacola)*. [Madrid?, c. 1720].

Although the Spaniards tried to establish settlements from Tampico to Apalache, their efforts failed, and the region fell into general neglect. This was changed, however, by ambitious Frenchmen, who sought to found a colony along the shores of the Gulf of Mexico during the latter part of the seventeenth century. Because of the intrusion of La Salle's expedition, the Spanish government moved to protect the borderlands by setting up missions in Texas and by occupying Pensacola Bay. Don Carlos de Sigüenza y Góngora took part in one of the investigative voyages to the Bay at the request of New Spain's Viceroy, the Count of Galve. Returning to Mexico City in 1693, he wrote this report on his reconnaissance in which he outlined plans for Pensacola's settlement and the defense of its coastline. This is the only recorded copy of this thirty-two-page pamphlet in the United States.

60.

COMPAÑÍA DE MARÍA SANTÍSIMA DE LA ENSEÑANZA DE MÉXICO. *Relacion historica de la fundacion de este Convento de Nuestra Señora del Pilar . . . y compendio de la vida y virtudes de* N.M.R.M. *Maria Ignacia Azlor y Echeverz su fundadora y patrona.* Mexico, 1793.

Women as well as men were called to settle the Spanish borderlands. The biography of the nun María Ignacia Azlor y Echeverz (1715–1767) recounts how she founded a convent dedicated to the education of young girls. María Ignacia Azlor y Echeverz (fig. 77) was the daughter of the Marquis of Aguayo, governor of Coahuila and Texas and one of the first settlers of the area. When she entered the convent, she brought with her the considerable fortune her family had made from the Mazapil silver mines.

In the eighteenth century, the road from the Franciscan mission at San Antonio to Sister María Ignacia's Convent of Nuestra Señora del Pilar was more than seven hundred miles long. Among the missions depicted on the 1764 map of the area (fig. 78) is that of San Antonio de Valero. It later became known as the Alamo, and was the site of the 1836 massacre led by the Mexican General Antonio López de Santa Anna.

FIG. 77. Portrait of María Ignacia Azlor y Echeverz, from COMPAÑÍA DE MARÍA SANTÍSIMA DE LA ENSEÑANZA, *Relación histórica.*

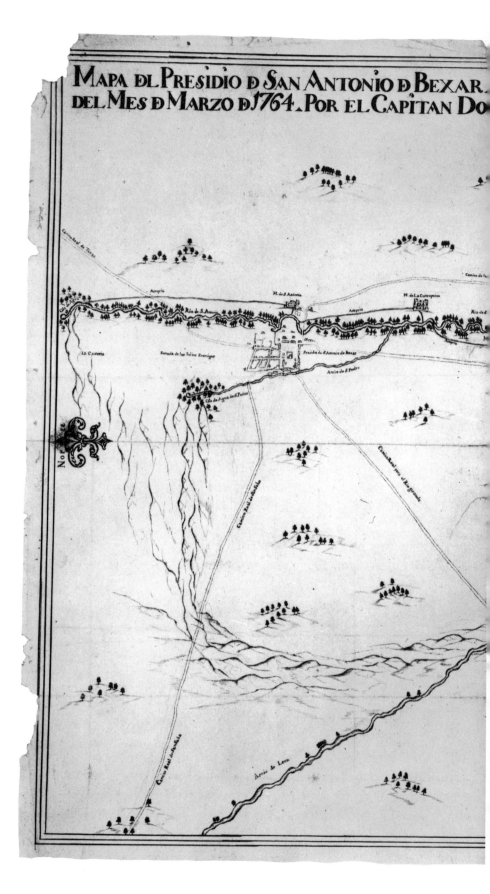

MAPA ᴅᴇʟ PRESIDIO ᴅ SAN ANTONIO ᴅ BEXAR.
ᴅᴇʟ MES ᴅ MARZO ᴅ 1764. POR EL CAPITAN DO

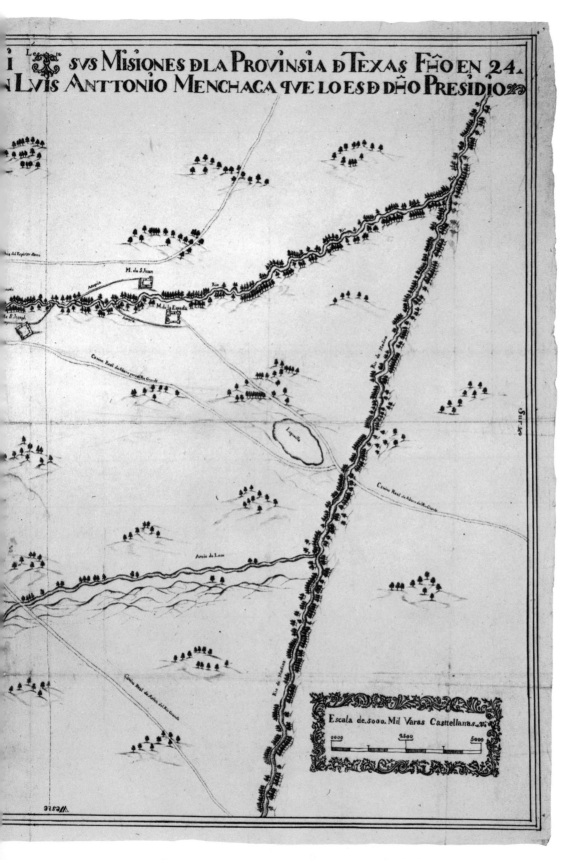

FIG. 78. LUIS ANTONIO MENCHACA, *Mapa del presidio de San Antonio.*

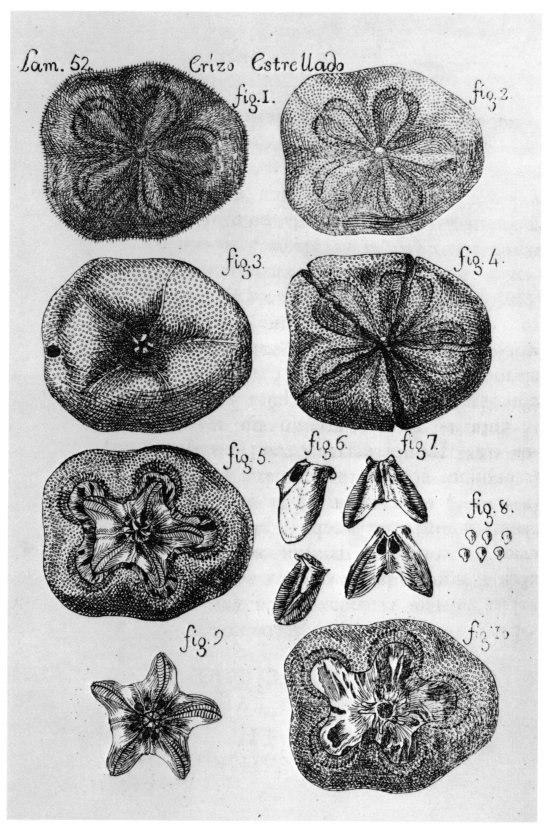

FIG. 79. Sand dollars, from ANTONIO PARRA, *Descripción de diferentes piezas de historia natural* (enlarged).

Other Spanish Possessions in America

THE VICEROYALTY OF NEW GRANADA

61.

PEDRO MASÚSTEGUI. *Arte de construccion*. Santa Fé [de Bogotá], 1784.

By the eighteenth century, Spain's empire had become too cumbersome to be ruled from Mexico City and Lima, and the Bourbon kings created new territorial and administrative divisions, including the Viceroyalty of New Granada (1717). By then, printing presses were in operation in many parts of the Spanish American colonies, not just in the old viceregal centers of political or religious activity.

The Jesuits brought the first press to Bogotá, the major city of New Granada, but their expulsion in 1767 interrupted its operations. In 1777 Antonio de los Monteros, who had established a print shop in Cartagena some years earlier, relocated in Bogotá and took over some of the equipment left by the Society of Jesus. His press printed Masústegui's *Arte de construcción*, an instructional manual on the methods of Latin translation that had been published in Seville in 1734.

THE CAPTAINCY-GENERAL OF CUBA

62.

ANTONIO PARRA. *Descripcion de diferentes piezas de historia natural*. Havana, 1787.

Immediately following the discovery of America, the island colonies of the Caribbean were the center of activity, but they were neglected soon after the conquest of Mexico and Peru. Even Cuba, the most important and the wealthiest, probably did not have a fully operational press before the eighteenth century. Among the printers who practiced their trade in Havana was Esteban José Boloña, whose works are noted for their exceptional quality. The plates he prepared for the *Descripción de diferentes piezas de historia natural* (figs. 79 and 80), one of the first books produced on his press, are good examples of his talent for design, and the recognition he received subsequently won him an appointment as printer for the Royal Navy.

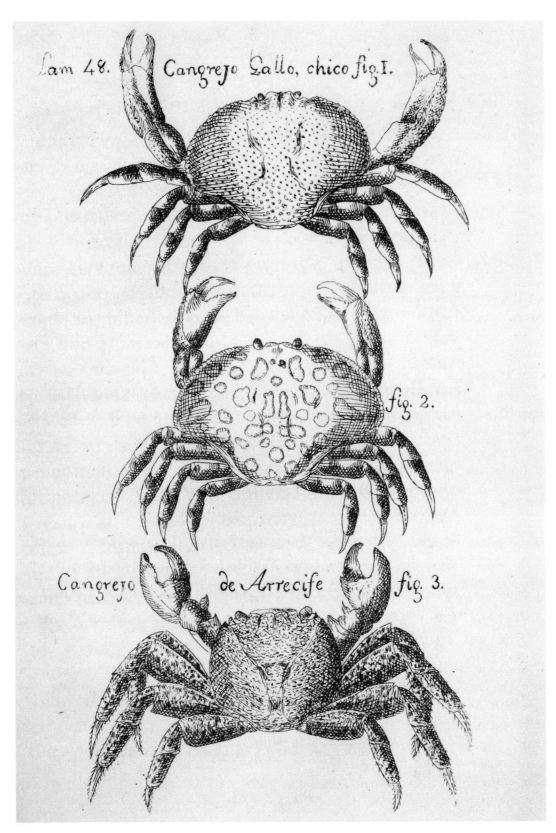

FIG. 80. Crabs, from ANTONIO PARRA, *Descripción de diferentes piezas de historia natural* (enlarged).

63.

VENEZUELA. *Constitucion federal, para los estados de Venezuela.* Caracas, 1812.

During the first decade of the nineteenth century, Spain was unable to maintain its firm grip on outlying areas of the Spanish colonies such as Venezuela. Caracas was a center of revolutionary activity, and the printing press played an important role in the region's separation from the empire and the establishment of its new government.

On July 5, 1811, Venezuela declared its independence from Spain, and the following year this Constitution was published. The new republic suffered several setbacks, however, with a devastating earthquake and serious political divisions among the country's leaders, but Simón Bolívar soon emerged as its new commander-in-chief. He was chosen to lead the rebel forces against the royalists in Peru, and in 1824 he finally attained the victory that would free South America from Spanish domination.

This is the only recorded copy of the forty-page *Constitución federal* of 1812 in the United States.

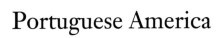

Portuguese America

THE BOOK AND PRINTING IN
PORTUGUESE AMERICA

NUMEROUS FACTORS distinguish the pattern of colonization in Brazil from that of the territories conquered by the Spanish in the New World. Although strategic and religious considerations were important, the Portuguese established a colony in South America primarily because they wished to tap the region's economic potential. Various kinds of tropical wood attracted entrepreneurs to the Brazilian coast, and it was hoped that the demand for this commodity might replace a declining trade with India.

In addition to developing a thriving lumber industry, the Portuguese carved large plantations, or *fazendas*, out of the wild Brazilian forest, on which they produced rice, sugar, and other agricultural products for export. These plantations, rather than the towns and cities, became the early centers of colonial society. Indian civilizations, such as those found in Peru and Mexico, did not exist in Brazil, and the Portuguese colonists sought to enslave rather than assimilate the scattered tribes they encountered.

The pattern of colonization in Brazil and the character of the Indian population influenced the early development of printing and bookmaking there. It was difficult to govern a sparse, widely-scattered, often illiterate population dependent for the most part on the powerful landowners. As a result, relatively few books were imported, and the authorities believed that a printing press in the colony might threaten the established order. Brazil did not support a flourishing printing and publishing enterprise until external circumstances transformed Rio de Janeiro into the capital of the empire.

By the beginning of the eighteenth century, substantial urban populations were developing, and Salvador da Bahia was the second largest city in the Portuguese empire, after Lisbon. In 1807, when Napoleon's troops invaded the Iberian peninsula, the Portuguese court and bureaucracy, with the help of the English, were able to escape capture by fleeing to Brazil and bringing with them the principal instruments of government.

As the French army advanced on Lisbon, the National Library was placed on board ships waiting in the harbor. Printing equipment, if not loaded aboard then, was soon acquired by Prince Regent João's government-in-exile. In 1808, the Royal Printing

Office was established, and Brazil's first newspaper, the *Gazeta do Rio de Janeiro*, was published the same year. Although the Portuguese government returned to Lisbon in 1821, the cultural and intellectual activity stimulated by the court's presence did not cease. On the contrary, it grew with the output of the press, contributing to the formation of opinion leading to Brazil's declaration of independence the following year.

FIG. 81. ANTONIO DE ARAUJO, *Catecismo brasílico*.

Brazil

64.

JESUITS. *Avisi particolari delle Indie di Portugallo*. Rome, 1552.

In 1549, João III took decisive measures to establish Portuguese control over Brazil by sending a group of settlers to the colony under the leadership of Captain-General Tomé de Souza. Among its members were Father Manoel da Nóbrega and five companions, the first Jesuits to arrive in America after the Society's founding in 1540. Under orders from Ignatius Loyola himself, missionaries throughout the world were to report on the progress of their work and to take note of unusual plants and animals that flourished in their exotic surroundings. Because of the general interest in the letters sent to Loyola, they were edited and published in Rome. In 1552 the first report appeared with news of the Brazilian mission. This is the only copy of this work recorded in the United States.

65.

ANTONIO DE ARAUJO (1566–1632). *Catecismo brasilico de doutrina christãa*. Lisbon, 1686.

The arrival of the Jesuits marked the beginning of organized Christianity in Brazil, and the Society's progress was the most dynamic of any religious order until its expulsion from Portugal and its South American colony in 1759. In contrast to the Jesuits in other parts of the world, however, the missionaries to Brazil did not have access to a press and consequently depended on printers in Lisbon to supply them with religious works such as this extremely rare catechism (fig. 81).

The Jesuits were the principal agents for the transfer of European culture to the Indians. They established mission villages (*reduções*), where they founded many of their schools and libraries. The Jesuits' effectiveness in protecting the Indians from slavery brought them into conflict with powerful *fazendeiros*, who supported the Society's banishment. Lists of Jesuit property seized at the time of their expulsion attest to the excellence of their libraries. The largest was that of Rio de Janeiro's Jesuit College.

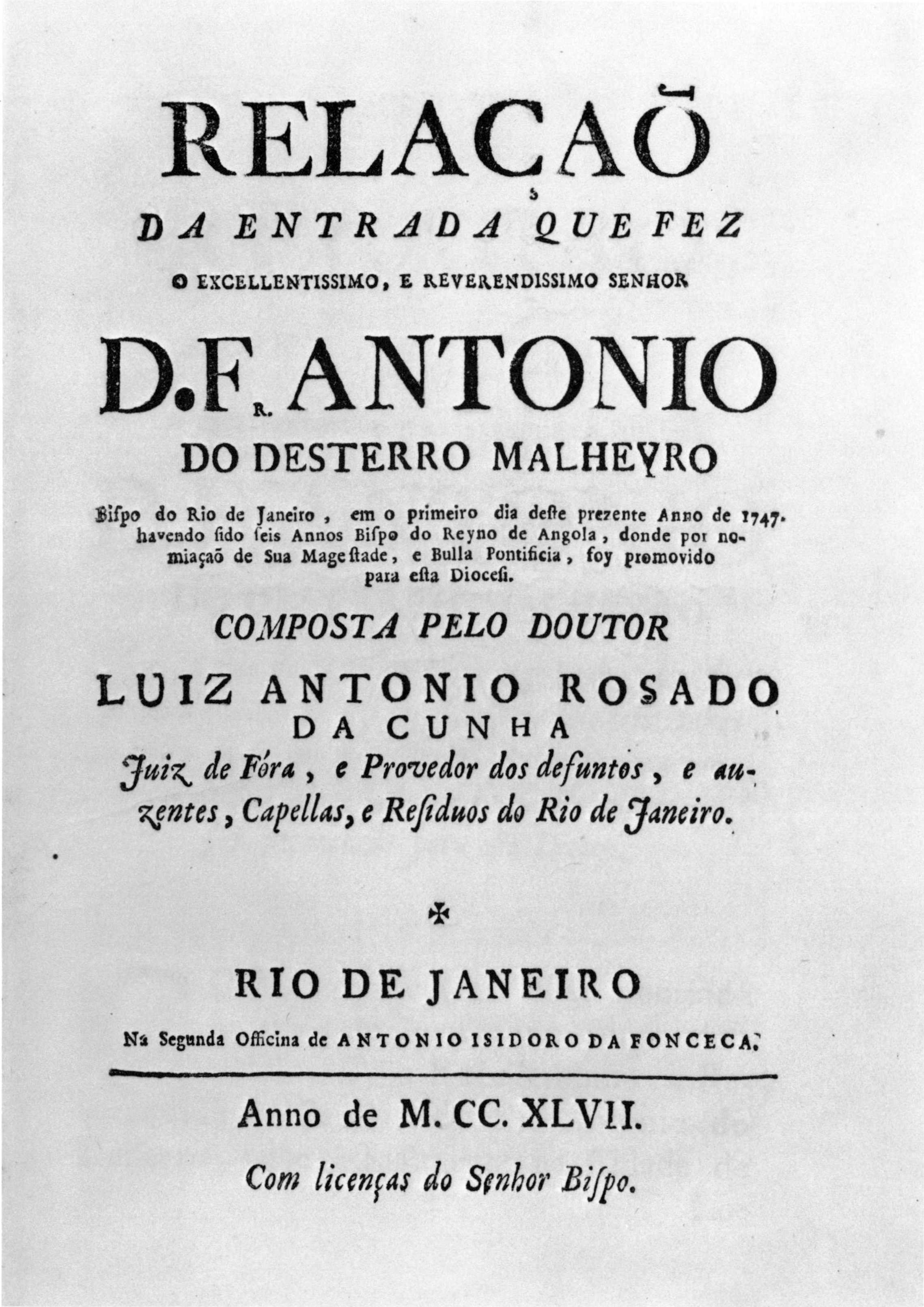

RELAÇAÕ

DA ENTRADA QUE FEZ

O EXCELLENTISSIMO, E REVERENDISSIMO SENHOR

D.F. ANTONIO

DO DESTERRO MALHEYRO

Bifpo do Rio de Janeiro, em o primeiro dia defte prezente Anno de 1747.
havendo fido feis Annos Bifpo do Reyno de Angola, donde por nomiaçaõ de Sua Mageftade, e Bulla Pontificia, foy promovido
para efta Diocefi.

COMPOSTA PELO DOUTOR

LUIZ ANTONIO ROSADO
DA CUNHA

Juiz de Fóra , e Provedor dos defuntos , e au-
zentes , Capellas, e Refiduos do Rio de Janeiro.

✠

RIO DE JANEIRO

Na Segunda Officina de ANTONIO ISIDORO DA FONCECA.

___

Anno de M. CC. XLVII.

Com licenças do Senhor Bifpo.

FIG. 82. LUIS ANTÓNIO ROSADA DA CUNHA, *Relaçaõ da entrada* (enlarged).

66.

LUIS ANTÓNIO ROSADO DA CUNHA. *Relaçaõ da entrada que fez o excellentissimo, e reverendissimo senhor D. Fr. Antonio do Desterro Malheyro*. Rio de Janeiro, [1747].

Although several historians suggest that a printing press was in operation in Recife, initially under the direction of the Dutch and later during the administration of the Portuguese governor Francisco de Castro Moraes, the first press for which definite proof exists is that of António Isidoro da Fonseca in Rio de Janeiro. He had established a fine reputation as a printer in Lisbon before coming to Brazil and is noted for his publication of Barbosa Machado's *Biblioteca lusitana*, a pioneering reference work in Portuguese bibliography. His reasons for coming to the New World are unclear; it is known, however, that he was in some economic difficulties and that the Inquisition was also investigating several of his publications.

Fonseca produced very few works on his press in Rio, for he was ordered by royal officials to close his shop in 1747, the same year that he began printing. Cunha's *Relaçaõ* is believed to be the first book printed in Brazil (fig. 82), and only six copies of it are known to exist at the present time. It was not, however, the first book to be printed in Portuguese in the New World. A priest in New Spain, Father João Bauptista Morelli de Castelnovo, wrote *Dom. Luzeiro Evangelico* to support the Church's evangelizing efforts in Asia, and it was published in Mexico in 1710.

67.

LUÍS DE CAMÕES (1524? – 1580). *Os Lusiadas*. Lisbon, 1572.

Much information regarding the composition and size of libraries in colonial Brazil has been gathered from legal documents that enumerate items of seized or taxed property. A frequent work listed in these inventories is that of the epic poet Luís de Camões, Portuguese literature's most prominent figure. After attending the University of Coimbra, he began a tumultuous period in his life that took him all over the world and brought him into constant conflict with ecclesiastical and government authorities. In 1553, he was released from prison and required to leave Portugal for the Orient.

His travels to India took him over the sea route followed by the navigator Vasco da Gama, the first European to arrive there by ship. This momentous journey, from which the Portuguese empire would emerge, became the central theme of Camões's epic. His interpretation of the event was much influenced by the works of Virgil and Ariosto. In 1570 he returned to Portugal where his verses were published two years later (fig. 83). *Os Lusiadas* won immediate acclaim and is considered one of the greatest epic poems of world literature. At the end of Canto x, Vasco da Gama is described as he contemplates the Portuguese development of South America and predicts that the colony will be named Brazil because of the red brazilwood growing there.

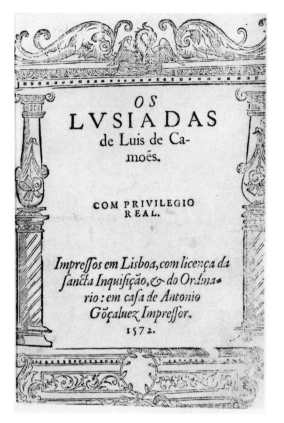

FIG. 83. LUÍS DE CAMOÉS, *Os Lusiadas*.   FIG. 84. MIGUEL DÍAS PIMENTA, *Noticias*.

68.

MIGUEL DÍAS PIMENTA (*c.* 1661–1715). *Noticias do que he o achaque do bicho*. Lisbon, 1707.

The threat posed by the Brazilian environment to the health of colonists was a matter of great concern and prompted the publication of a number of works on tropical medicine. In 1685 there was an outbreak of yellow fever in Pernambuco, which spread to Rio de Janeiro the following year. The account of the epidemic, by a Brazilian physician, was the first based on clinical observations to be written in the Portuguese colony (fig. 84). This copy of the work is unique in the United States.

69.

TOMÁS ANTÔNIO GONZAGA (1744–1807?). *Marilia de Dirceo*. Lisbon, 1819–[1820]

The metropolis of Vila Rica (the former capital of Minas Gerais province and now the city of Ouro Prêto) was a center for the arts by the middle of the eighteenth century. It became a gathering place for members of Brazil's intelligentsia who were primarily responsible for the colony's cultural achievements. During the latter part of the eighteenth century, they became the leaders of the *Inconfidência mineira*, a movement advocating independence from Portugal.

Among the prominent poets residing in Vila Rica was Tomás Antônio Gonzaga, who was born in Portugal of Brazilian parents. The tragic story of his love for Maria Dorotéia is told in his *Marilia de Dirceo*, and it achieved an immediate success unprecedented in the early literary history of the colony. There was no press in Brazil when the work was completed, so the manuscript was sent to Portugal for publication (fig. 85). Because sales were so brisk, four editions were printed in Lisbon between 1792 and 1800, and it would also be the first literary work printed by the Impressão Regia in Brazil.

70.

JOSÉ BASILIO DA GAMA (1740–1795). *O Uraguay.* Lisbon, 1769.

Brazil's first epic poet, José Basilio da Gama, was born in Minas Gerais and educated at the Jesuit College in Rio de Janeiro. Although he considered becoming a member of the Society of Jesus during his youth, before the Society's expulsion, he was to change his stance as anti-Jesuit sentiment became politically essential. Portugal's Prime Minister, the Marquis of Pombal, led the campaign against the Jesuits, and the poet endeavored to win his favor by advocating his policies.

Gama's five-canto poem contains an account of the campaign to put down an Indian revolt allegedly inspired by the Jesuits. The uprising took place in the buffer state of Sacramento, present-day Uruguay. *O Uraguay* is recognized as one of the outstanding works of early Brazilian literature, and it anticipates the emergence of certain Romantic themes, such as the "noble savage" and the cult of nature. Gama's work was one of the first to be published by Portugal's government press or Impressão Regia, which Pombal had established the previous year (fig. 86).

71.

BRAZIL. *Decreto. Tendo-me constado, que os prélos, que se achão nesta capital.* [Rio de Janeiro, 1811].

The period of exile for the Portuguese crown and government in Brazil brought many changes to the colony, among them the installation of a printing press which quickly became an indispensable tool of administration. In 1808, the authorization for printing was officially granted, and the Impressão Regia was established in Rio.

The origin of the equipment used to set up this government print shop has not been firmly established. One account claims that the new presses and type had arrived from

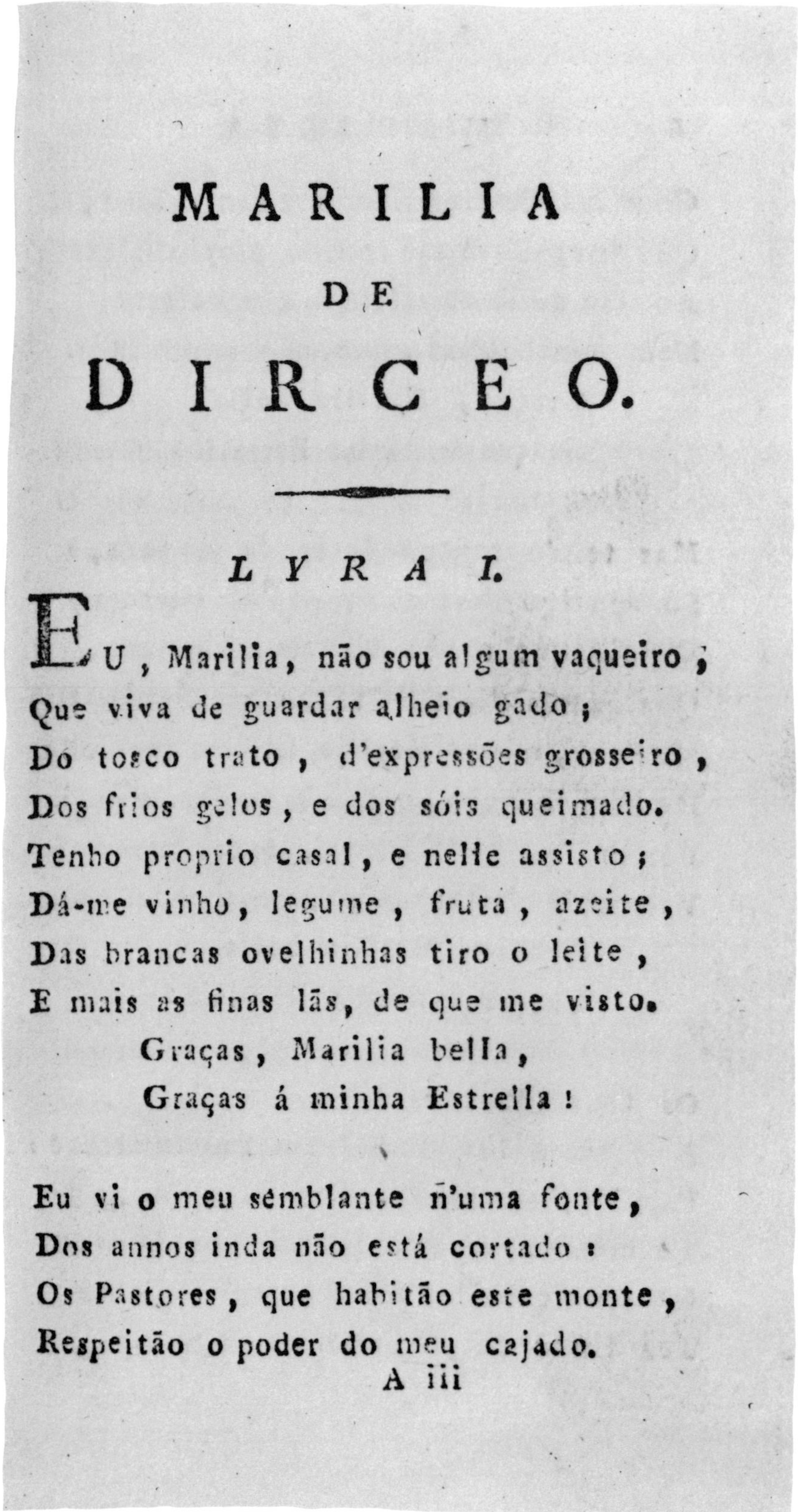

MARILIA

DE

DIRCEO.

———————

EU, Marilia, não sou algum vaqueiro,
Que viva de guardar alheio gado;
Do tosco trato, d'expressões grosseiro,
Dos frios gelos, e dos sóis queimado.
Tenho proprio casal, e nelle assisto;
Dá-me vinho, legume, fruta, azeite,
Das brancas ovelhinhas tiro o leite,
E mais as finas lãs, de que me visto.
    Graças, Marilia bella,
    Graças á minha Estrella!

Eu vi o meu semblante n'uma fonte,
Dos annos inda não está cortado:
Os Pastores, que habitão este monte,
Respeitão o poder do meu cajado.

A iii

FIG. 85. TOMÁS ANTÔNIO GONZAGA, *Marilia de Dirceo* (enlarged).

O URAGUAY
POEMA
DE
JOSÉ BASILIO DA GAMA
NA ARCADIA DE ROMA
TERMINDO SIPILIO
DEDICADO
AO ILL.MO E EXC.MO SENHOR
FRANCISCO XAVIER
DE MENDONÇA FURTADO
SECRETARIO DE ESTADO
DE
S. MAGESTADE FIDELISSIMA
&c. &c. &c.

LISBOA
NA REGIA OFFICINA TYPOGRAFICA
ANNO MDCCLXIX
Com licença da Real Meza Cenforia.

FIG. 86. JOSÉ BASILIO DA GAMA,
O Uraguay.

DECRETO.

Tendo-Me constado, que os Prélos, que se achão nesta Capital, erão os destinados para a Secretaria de Estado dos Negocios Estrangeiros, e da Guerra; e Attendendo à necessidade, que ha da Officina de Impressão nestes Meus Estados: Sou servido, que a Caza, onde elles se estabelecerão, sirva interinamente de Impressão Regia, onde se imprimão exclusivamente toda a Legislação, e Papeis Diplomaticos, que emanarem de qualquer Repartição do Meu Real Serviço; e se possão imprimir todas, e quaesquer outras Obras; ficando interinamente pertencendo o seu governo, e administração à mesma Secretaria. Dom Rodrigo de Souza Coutinho, Do Meu Conselho de Estado, Ministro, e Secretario de Estado dos Negocios Estrangeiros, e da Guerra o tenha assim entendido, e procurará dar ao emprego da Officina a maior extensão, e lhe dará todas as Instrucções, e Ordens necessarias, e participará a este respeito a todas as Estações o que mais convier ao Meu Real Serviço. Palacio do Rio de Janeiro em treze de Maio de mil oitocentos e oito.

Com a Rubrica do PRINCIPE REGENTE N. S.

Regist.

Na Impressão Regia.

FIG. 87. BRAZIL, *Decreto. Tendo-me constado.*

England just prior to the French invasion and were still on the docks in Lisbon at the time of the court's evacuation. As the last ships were leaving the harbor, the foreign secretary, António de Araujo Azevedo, had them loaded onto a frigate for shipment to Brazil.

The one-page decree establishing the government press appeared in Volume 1 of the *Codigo Brasiliense*, a collection of laws (fig. 87).

72.

MANUEL FERREIRA DE ARAUJO GUIMARÃES (1777–1838). *Elementos de astronomia.* Rio de Janeiro, [1814].

The Impressão Regia enjoyed a monopoly over printing in Rio for fourteen years. During that time more than twelve hundred items were produced, and the press's activity increased considerably in 1821 when censorship was abolished in Brazil. Although most of the products of the press consisted of official documents, religious works, and broadsides, books used for instruction in the city's schools were also printed.

$$\frac{360c'}{2\pi} = b\left\{1 - a(1-3\text{fen}^2\,\phi')\right\}.$$

Dividindo as duas equações, membro por membro, virá

$$\frac{c}{c'} = \frac{1-a(1-3\text{fen}^2\,\phi)}{1-a(1-3\text{fen}^2\,\phi')},$$

equação em que não ha mais incognita que o achatamento a, e que dá, desprezando o quadrado de a

$$\frac{c}{c'} = 1 - 3a(\text{fen}^2\,\phi' - \text{fen}^2\,\phi);$$

e donde se tira finalmente

$$a = \frac{c'-c}{3c(\text{fen}^2\,\phi' - \text{fen}^2\,\phi)}.$$

75. Tomemos para exemplo o gráo medido no equador por *Bouguer*, e o de França medido por *Delambre* e *Mechain*. Teremos neste caso

$$c = 56753^t \ldots \phi = 0, \; c' = 57018,42, \phi' = 46°,2.$$

O que dá

$$c' - c = 265^t\,42., \text{fen}\,\phi' = 0, \; 721753 .. \text{fen}\,\phi = 0, \text{ e}$$

$$a = \frac{265,42}{88696,02} = \frac{1}{334}.$$

76. Conhecido a, tornemos á equação

$$\frac{360c}{2\pi} = b\left\{1 - a(1-3\text{fen}^2\,\phi)\right\};$$

fazendo $\phi = 0$, ella fica

$$\frac{360c}{2\pi} = b(1-a); \text{ donde vem}$$

$$b = \frac{180.c}{\pi(1-a)},$$

e desprezando as segundas potencias de a

$$b = \frac{180.c(1+a)}{\pi}.$$

Temos tambem $a = b(1+a)$. Por tanto ficaráõ conhecidos os valores de a, e b, isto, he os dous eixos do ellipsoide.
Pondo em lugar de a e c os seus valores, se acha

$$b = 3261443^t$$
$$a = 3271208$$
$$a - b = 9765.$$

77. Comparando do mesmo modo o gráo da *Laponia* com o do equador, teremos o achatamento $\frac{1}{325}$, e para a e b valores pouco differentes dos precedentes. Em todos os calculos, em que entrar o achatamento da terra, tomaremos sempre $\frac{1}{334}$.

78. Empreguemos tambem para examinarmos a figura da terra os comprimentos observados dos pendulos de segundos, tomando por unidade o de Paris.

5

FIG. 88. Equations, from MANUEL FERREIRA DE ARAUJO GUIMARÃES, *Elementos de astronomia*.

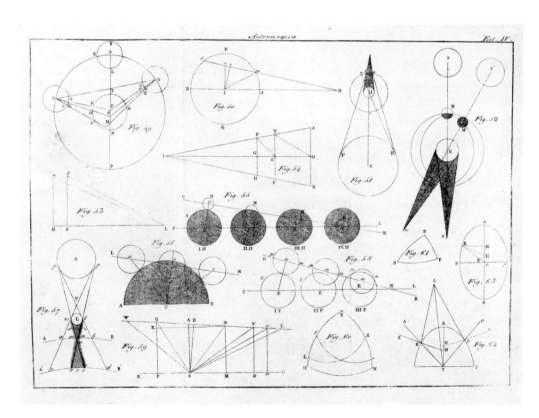

FIG. 89. Figures, from MANUEL FERREIRA DE ARAUJO GUIMARÃES, *Elementos de astronomia*.

Among them was Araujo Guimarães's basic text on astronomy, which he prepared for the students of the Royal Military Academy (figs. 88 and 89). This is the only copy of the work recorded in the United States.

73.

JOHN LUCCOCK. *Notes on Rio de Janeiro, and the southern parts of Brazil.* London, 1820.

By the beginning of the eighteenth century Portugal and England were closely allied. Englishmen were allowed to travel freely in Brazil after the arrival there of the Portuguese court, and they made many contributions to the colony's early progress.

John Luccock was among the merchants who took up residence in Brazil, and his ten-year stay there is recounted in his *Notes*. The work contains information about the Paul Martin family's legitimate book trade and provides evidence on the flow of contraband books to Brazil. Luccock also reported that the Prince Regent secretly supported the establishment of freedom of the press, but no such decree was issued. Publishers of Portuguese works, therefore, continued to flourish in London and Paris.

SELECTED SOURCES

for the Study of The Book in the Americas

GENERAL

AVILA MARTEL, Alamiro de. *José Toribio Medina, historiógrafo de América, 1852–1952.* Montevideo: Universidad de la República Oriental del Uruguay, Facultad de Humanidades y Ciencias, 1952.

BROMSEN, Maury A., ed. *José Toribio Medina, Humanist of the Americas.* Washington, D.C., 1960.

CLINE, Howard. *Guide to Ethnohistorical Sources, Part Three.* Vol. 14 of the *Handbook of Middle American Indians,* edited by Robert Wauchope. Austin: University of Texas Press, 1975.

FELIÚ CRUZ, Guillermo. *José Toribio Medina, historiador y bibliógrafo de América.* Santiago de Chile: Editorial Nascimiento, 1952.

—— *Medina, el hombre.* (An English translation of the address inaugurating the Medina centennial celebration.) Washington, D.C., 1952.

FERNÁNDEZ DEL CASTILLO, Francisco. *Libros y libreros en el siglo xvi.* Mexico, 1914.

JONES, Tom B. "The Classics in Colonial Hispanic America." *Transactions of the American Philological Association* 70 (1939): 37–45.

LEONARD, Irving A. *Romances of Chivalry in the Spanish Indies with Some* Registros *of Shipment of Books to the Spanish Colonies.* Berkeley: University of California Press, 1933.

LEVENE, Ricardo. *Homenaje a la memoria de José Toribio Medina en el centenario de su nacimiento.* Buenos Aires, 1952.

MEDINA, José Toribio. *Historia de la imprenta en los antiguos dominios españoles de América y Oceanía.* Santiago de Chile: Fondo Histórico y Bibliográfico José Toribio Medina, 1958.

MILLARES CARLO, Agustín. *Introducción a la historia del libro y de las bibliotecas.* Mexico: Fondo de Cultura Económica, 1971.

MOHLER, Stephen C. "Publishing in Colonial Spanish America: An Overview." *Revista Interamericana de Bibliografía* 28 (1978): 259–273.

OLAGUIBEL, Manuel de. *Impresiones célebres y libros raros.* Mexico: Imprenta del "Socialista" de M. López, 1878.

RODRÍGUEZ MARÍN, Francisco. *El 'Quijote' y Don Quijote en América.* Madrid: Hernando, 1911.

SCHAIBLE, Carl H. *Bibliografía de José Toribio Medina.* Santiago de Chile: Sociedad de Bibliófilos Chilenos, 1952.

THOMPSON, Lawrence S. "Book Illustration in Colonial Spanish America." In *Book Illustration: Papers Presented at the Third Rare Book Conference of the American Literary Association,* edited by Frances Joan Brewer. Berlin: Gebruder Mann Verlag, 1963.

—— "The Libraries of Colonial Spanish America." *The Library Binder* 138 (1963): 6–13.

TORRE REVELLO, José. *El libro, la imprenta y el periodismo en América durante la dominación española.* New York: B. Franklin, 1973.

—— "Merchandise Shipped by the Spaniards to America (1534–1586)." *Hispanic American Historical Review* 23 (1943): 773–781.

—— *Orígenes de la imprenta en España y su desarrollo en América Española.* Buenos Aires: Institución Cultural Española, 1940.

WINSHIP, George Parker. *The Printing Press in South America.* Providence: The John Carter Brown Library, 1912.

WOODBRIDGE, Hensley C., and Lawrence S. Thompson. *Printing in Colonial Spanish America.* Troy, N.Y.: Whitston Publishing Company, 1976.

THE VICEROYALTY OF NEW SPAIN

Mexico

BAUDOT, Georges. "La biblioteca de los evangelizadores de México." *Historia Mexicana* 17 (1968): 610–617.

BENÍTEZ, José R. *Historia gráfica de la Nueva España.*
Mexico: Cámara Oficial Española de Comercio, 1939.

BERISTAIN DE SOUZA, José Mariano. *Biblioteca hispanoamericana septentrional.* 3 vols. Mexico, 1816–1821.

BURRUS, Ernest J. "Two Lost Mexican Books of the

Sixteenth Century." *Hispanic American Historical Review* 37 (1957): 330–339.

CARREÑO, Alberto María. *Don Fray Juan de Zumárraga, teólogo y editor, humanista e inquisidor.* Mexico: Jus, 1950.

—— "The Books of Don Fray Juan de Zumárraga." *The Americas* 5 (1949): 311–330.

—— "La imprenta y la Inquisición en el siglo xvi." *Revista de Revistas* 15 (1924): 19–21.

CASTAÑEDA, Carlos Eduardo. *The Beginning of Printing in America.* New York, 1939.

GARCÍA ICAZBALCETA, Joaquín. *Bibliografía mexicana del siglo xvi: Catálogo razonado de libros impresos en México de 1539 a 1600.* Edited by Agustín Millares Carlo. Mexico: Fondo de Cultura Económica, 1954.

—— *Don Fray Juan de Zumárraga, primer obispo y arzobispo de México: Estudio biográfico.* 2 vols. Mexico: Andrade y Morales, 1881.

GEIGER, Maynard. "The Library of the Apostolic College of San Fernando, Mexico, in the Eighteenth and Nineteenth Centuries." *The Americas* 7 (1951): 425–434.

GONZÁLEZ OBREGÓN, Luis. *Epoca colonial. México viejo; noticias históricas, tradiciones, leyendas y costumbres.* Paris and Mexico: Librería de la viuda de C. Bouret, 1900.

—— *Libros y libreros en el siglo xvi.* Mexico: Archivo General de la Nación, 1914.

GREEN, Otis H., and Irving A. Leonard. "On the Mexican Book Trade in 1600: A Chapter in Cultural History." *Hispanic Review* 9 (1941): 1–40.

GREENLEAF, Richard E. *The Mexican Inquisition of the Sixteenth Century.* Albuquerque: University of New Mexico Press, 1969.

—— *Zumárraga and the Mexican Inquisition.* Washington, D.C.: Academy of American Franciscan History, 1961.

IGUÍNIZ, Juan B. *La imprenta en la Nueva España.* Mexico: Porrúa, 1938.

—— *La imprenta en la Nueva Galicia, 1793–1821. Apuntes bibliográficos.* Mexico: Imprenta del Museo Nacional de Arqueología, Historia y Etnología, 1911.

IGUÍNIZ, Juan B., Alberto María Carreño, and Federico Gómez Orozco. "Dictámen de la Academia Mexicana de la Historia Correspondiente de la Real de Madrid acerca del primer libro impreso en América según el señor Francisco Vindel." *Memorias de la Academia Mexicana de la Historia* 13 (1954).

IHMOFF CABRERA, Jesús. *Catálogo de incunables de la Biblioteca Nacional de México.* Mexico: Universidad Nacional Autónoma de México, 1968.

LEA, Henry Charles. *The Inquisition in the Spanish Dependencies.* New York: Macmillan, 1908.

LEÓN, Nicolás. *La imprenta en México.* Ann Arbor: University of Michigan Press, 1966.

LEONARD, Irving A. *Baroque Times in Old Mexico.* Ann Arbor: University of Michigan Press, 1966.

LINGA, Carlos R. "Los primeros tipógrafos en la Nueva España y sus precursores europeos." In *IV Centenario de la imprenta en México, la primera de América. Conferencias sustentadas en su conmemoración.* Mexico: Sociedad de Libreros Mexicanos, 1939.

MATHES, W. Michael. *Un centro cultural novogalaico: La biblioteca del convento de San Francisco de Guadalajara en 1610.* Mexico: Instituto Cultural Cabanas, 1986.

—— *La biblioteca de San Francisco de Guadalajara en el siglo xvi.* Guadalajara, Mexico: In press.

—— *La imprenta en Santiago Tlatelolco.* Mexico: In press.

—— *Mexico on Stone: Mexican Nineteenth-Century Lithography.* Book Club of California: In press.

—— *Santa Cruz de Tlatelolco: La primera biblioteca académica de América.* Mexico: Secretaría de Relaciones Exteriores, 1982.

MAZA, Francisco de la. *Enrico Martínez, cosmógrafo e impresor de España.* Mexico, 1943.

MEDINA, José Toribio. *Introducción de la imprenta en América.* Santiago de Chile: Imprenta Cervantes, 1910.

—— *La imprenta en Guadalajara de México (1793–1821): Notas bibliográficas.* Santiago de Chile: Imprenta Elzeviriana, 1904.

—— *La imprenta en la Puebla de los Angeles.* Santiago de Chile: Imprenta Cervantes, 1908.

—— *La imprenta en México (1539–1821).* Santiago de Chile: Impreso en casa del autor, 1908–1912.

—— *La imprenta en Oaxaca (1720–1820): Notas bibliográficas.* Santiago de Chile: Imprenta Elzeviriana, 1904; reprinted in Amsterdam: N. Israel, 1964.

—— *La imprenta en Veracruz (1784–1821): Notas bibliográficas.* Santiago de Chile: Imprenta Elzeviriana, 1904; reprinted in Amsterdam: N. Israel, 1964.

MILLARES CARLO, Agustín, and Julián Calvo. *Juan Pablos, primero impresor que a esta tierra vino.* Mexico: Gabriel Saldivar, 1953.

NIXON, Howard M. "Mexican Gold-Tooled Binding, c. 1597." In *Sixteenth-Century Bookbindings in the Pierpont Morgan Library*. New York: The Pierpont Morgan Library, 1971.

OLAGUIBEL, Manuel de. *Impresiones célebres y libros raros*. Mexico: Imprenta del "Socialista" de M. López, 1878.

PEÑALOSA, Fernando. *The Mexican Book Industry*. New York: Scarecrow Press, 1957.

RODRÍGUEZ-BUCKINGHAM, Antonio. "The Arm of Spain: Content Analysis of the Materials Printed in Mexico and Peru in the Sixteenth Century." In *Latin American Studies in Europe*, edited by A. H. Jordan. Austin: University of Texas Press, 1979.

—— "The First Forty Years of the Book Industry in Sixteenth Century Mexico." In *Iberian Colonies, New World Societies: Essays in Memory of Charles Gibson*, edited by R. Garner and W. P. Taylor. Privately printed. University Park, Penna.: At the Pennsylvania State University, 1986.

SALAS, Rafael. *Marcas de fuego de las antiguas bibliotecas mexicanas*. Mexico: Monografías Bibliográficas Mexicanas, 1925.

SCHONS, Dorothy. *Book Censorship in New Spain*. Austin: University of Texas Press, 1949.

STECK, Francis Borgia. *El primer colegio de América, Santa Cruz de Tlatelolco*. Mexico: Centro de Estudios Franciscanos, 1944.

STOLS, Alexandre A. M. *Antonio de Espinosa, el segundo impresor mexicano*. Mexico: Universidad Nacional Autónoma de México, Instituto Bibliográfico Mexicano, 1962.

—— *Pedro Ocharte, el tercer impresor mexicano*. Mexico: Imprenta Nuevo Mundo, 1962.

TEIXIDOR, Felipe. *Ex libris y bibliotecas de México*. Mexico: Secretaría de Relaciones Exteriores, 1931.

VALTÓN, Emilio. "Algunas particularidades tipográficas de los impresos mexicanos del siglo xvi." In *IV Centenario de la imprenta en México, la primera de América. Conferencias sustentadas en su conmemoración*. Mexico: Sociedad de Libreros Mexicanos, 1939.

—— *Impresos mexicanos del siglo xvi (incunables mexicanos) en la Biblioteca Nacional de México, el Museo Nacional y el Archivo General de la Nación; con cincuenta y dos láminas; estudio bibliográfico precedido de una introducción sobre los orígenes de la imprenta en América*. Mexico: Imprenta Universitaria, 1935.

VINDEL, Francisco. *En papel de fabricación azteca fue impreso el primer libro en América: Apuntes que comprueban la falta de veracidad en un dictamen de la Academia Mexicana de la Historia*. Madrid, 1956.

—— *El primer libro impreso en América fué para el rezo del Santo Rosario. Méjico, 1532–1534. Facsímile, estudios y comentarios*. Madrid, 1953. *Apéndice*. Madrid, 1954.

WAGNER, Henry R. "Sixteenth-Century Mexican Imprints [and] Location Table of Mexican Sixteenth-Century Books." In *Bibliographical Essays: A Tribute to Wilberforce Eames*. Freeport, N.Y.: Books for Libraries Press, 1967.

WARREN, J. Benedict. "Writing the Language of Michoacán: Sixteenth-Century Franciscan Linguistics." In *Franciscan Presence in the Americas*, edited by Francisco Morales, O.F.M. Washington, D.C.: Academy of American Franciscan History, 1983.

WROTH, Lawrence C. *Some Reflections on the Book Arts in Early Mexico*. Cambridge, Mass., 1945.

ZEPEDA RINCÓN, Tomás. *La educación pública en la Nueva España en el siglo xvi*. Mexico, 1972.

ZULÁICA GARATE, Román. *Los franciscanos y la imprenta en México en el siglo xvi: Estudio bio-bibliográfico*. Mexico: Pedro Robredo, 1939.

Guatemala

DÍAZ, Victor Miguel. *Historia de la imprenta en Guatemala desde los tiempos de la colonia, hasta la época actual*. Guatemala: Tipografía Nacional, 1930.

MEDINA, José Toribio. *La imprenta en Guatemala (1660–1821)*. Santiago de Chile: Impreso en Casa Jilantor, 1910; reprinted in Amsterdam: N. Israel, 1964.

STOLS, Alexandre A. M. *La introducción de la imprenta en Guatemala*. Mexico: Universidad Nacional Autónoma de México, 1960.

VELA, David. *La imprenta en la Guatemala colonial*. Guatemala: Editorial del Ministerio de Educación Pública, 1960.

THE VICEROYALTY OF PERU

Peru

AVILA MARTEL, Alamiro de, ed. *La 'Pragmática sobre los diez días del año,' primera muestra tipográfica salida de las prensas de la América del Sur*. Santiago de Chile: Ediciones de la Universidad de Chile, 1984.

LEONARD, Irving A. "Best Sellers of the Lima Book

Trade, 1583." *Hispanic American Historical Review* 22 (1942): 5–33.

—— "*Don Quixote* and the Book Trade in Lima, 1606." *Hispanic American Historical Review* 8 (1940): 285–304.

—— "*Guzmán de Alfarache* in the Lima Book of Trade, 1613." *Hispanic Review* 11 (1943): 210–220.

—— "On the Cuzco Book Trade, 1606." *Hispanic Review* 9 (1941): 359–375.

MᶜMURTRIE, Douglas C. *The First Printing in South America.* Providence: The John Carter Brown Library, 1926.

MARQUES ABANTO, Alberto. "Don Antonio Ricardo, introductor de la imprenta en Lima; su testamento y codicilio." *Revista del Archivo Nacional del Perú* 19 (1955): 290–305.

MEDINA, José Toribio. *Diario de un tipógrafo yanqui (Samuel B. Johnston) en Chile y Perú.* Madrid: Editorial-América, 1919.

—— *La imprenta en Lima (1584–1824).* 4 vols. Santiago de Chile: Impreso y grabado en casa del autor, 1904–1907; reprinted in Amsterdam: N. Israel, 1965.

—— *La primera muestra tipográfica salida de la prensa de la América del Sur.* Santiago de Chile, 1916.

MIRÓ QUESADA, Aurelio. "La imprenta de Antonio Ricardo: La primera en América del Sur." *San Marcos, Nueva Epoca* 14 (1976): 3–26.

ROBERTS, W. "A Typographical Mystery." *Pan American Magazine* 34 (1922): 15–16.

RODRÍGUEZ-BUCKINGHAM, Antonio. "The Arm of Spain: Content Analysis of the Materials Printed in Mexico and Peru in the Sixteenth Century." In *Latin American Studies in Europe*, edited by A. H. Jordan. Austin: University of Texas Press, 1979.

—— "Colonial Peru and the Printing Press of Antonio Ricardo." Ph.D. diss., University of Michigan, 1977.

—— "The Establishment, Production, and Equip-

ment of the First Printing Shop in South America." *Harvard Library Bulletin* 26 (July, 1978): 342–354.

—— "First Printings of South America in the Harvard Library." *Harvard Library Bulletin* 16 (January, 1968): 38–48.

—— "The Renaissance in the New World: Printing in Colonial South America." *Explorations for Renaissance Culture* 10 (April, 1984): 67–79.

RODRÍGUEZ MOÑINO, A. R. "Como se publicaba un libro en Indias a principios del siglo xvii. Andanzas inquisitoriales de la *Ovandina*, crónica de linajes coloniales." *Tierra Firme*, 3–4 (1936).

Chile

AMUNÁTEGUI SOLAR, Domingo. "La primera imprenta chilena se debió a la Compañía de Jesús." *Revista Chilena de Historia y Geografía* 78 (1933): 82–87.

CANTER, Juan. "El material impresor de Haimhausen y el origen del arte de imprimir en Chile y en Córdoba." In *Segundo Congreso Internacional de Historia de América.* Buenos Aires, 1938.

FELIÚ CRUZ, Guillermo. *Bibliografía histórica de la imprenta en Santiago de Chile , 1818–1964.* Santiago de Chile: Talleres de la Editorial Nascimiento, 1964.

MEDINA, José Toribio. *Bibliografía de la imprenta en Santiago de Chile desde sus orígenes hasta febrero de 1817.* Santiago de Chile: Fondo Histórico y Bibliográfico José Toribio Medina, 1961.

—— *Diario de un tipógrafo yanqui (Samuel B. Johnston) en Chile y Perú.* Madrid: Editorial-América, 1919.

PEREIRA SALAS, Eugenio. "Don Mateo Arnaldo Hoevel." *Revista Chilena de Historia y Geografía* 97 (1940): 57–93.

SCHABILE, Carlos H. "Los orígenes de la imprenta en Chile." *El Mercurio* (Santiago de Chile), 6 November 1955.

THE VICEROYALTY OF RÍO DE LA PLATA

Argentina, Paraguay, and Uruguay

CANTER, Juan. "El material impresor de Haimhausen y el origen del arte de imprimir en Chile y en Córdoba." In *Segundo Congreso Internacional de Historia de América.* Buenos Aires, 1938.

FÚRLONG CÁRDIFF, Guillermo. *Bibliotecas argentinas durante la dominación hispánica.* Buenos Aires, 1944.

—— *Historia y bibliografía de las primeras imprentas rioplatenses, 1700–1850.* 3 vols. Buenos Aires: Editorial Guaranía, 1953–1959.

—— *Orígenes del arte tipográfico en la República Argentina.* Buenos Aires: Editorial Huarpes, 1947.

Colombia and Ecuador

CAUCA PRADA, Antonio. *Historia del periodismo colombiano*. Bogotá, 1968.

POSADA, Eduardo. *Bibliografía bogotana*. Bogotá: Imprenta de Arboleda y Valencia, 1917.

STOLS, Alexandre A. M. *Historia de la imprenta en el Ecuador, 1755–1830*. Quito: Casa de la Cultura Ecuatoriana, 1953.

Cuba

MEDINA, José Toribio. *La imprenta en La Habana (1707–1810)*. Santiago de Chile: Imprenta Elzeviriana, 1904; reprinted in Amsterdam: N. Israel, 1964.

Venezuela

DRENIKOFF, Ivan. *Impresos relativos a Venezuela desde el descubrimiento hasta 1821*. Caracas, 1978.

GRASES, Pedro. *Historia de la imprenta en Venezuela hasta el fin de la primera república (1812)*. Caracas: Ediciones de la Presidencia de la República, 1967.

MEDINA, José Toribio. *La imprenta en Caracas (1808–1821)*. Santiago de Chile, 1904; reprinted in Amsterdam: N. Israel, 1964.

MILLARES CARLO, Agustín. *La imprenta y el periodismo en Venezuela desde sus orígenes hasta mediados del siglo xix*. [Caracas]: Monte Avila, [1969].

BRAZIL

BARRETO, Dalmo Freira. "*De Brasiliae rebus pluribus*: O primeiro libro impresso no Brasil." *Revista do Instituto Histórico e Geográfico Brasileiro* 140 (314) (January/March 1977): 51–74.

BRANDENBERGER, Clemens. "Die ältesten brasilischen Drucke." In *Gutembergfestschrift zur Feier des 25. jährigen Bestehens des Gutembergmuseums in Mainz 1925*. Mainz, 1925.

BURNS, E. Bradford. "The Enlightenment in Two Colonial Brazilian Libraries." *Journal of the History of Ideas* 25 (1964): 430–438.

—— "The Intellectuals as Agents of Change and the Independence of Brazil, 1724–1822." In *From Colony to Nation: Essays on the Independence of Brazil*, edited by A.J.R. Russell-Wood. Baltimore: The Johns Hopkins University Press, 1975.

CÂNDIDO, Antônio [Antônio Cândido de Mello e Souza]. *Formação da literatura brasileira (momentos decisivos)*. 2a ed. rev. São Paulo: Livraria Martins, 1964.

CARVALHO, Alfredo Ferreira de. *Annaes da imprensa periodica pernambucana de 1821–1908*. Recife: Jornal do Recife, 1908.

CASTRO, Renato Berbet de. *A primeira imprensa da Bahia e suas publicações*. Salvador: Secretaria Estadual da Cultura, 1969.

COSTA, Francisco Augusto Pereira da. *Anais pernambucanos*. Vol. 1: *1493–1590*. Recife: Arquivo Publico Estadual, 1951.

DIEGUES JÚNIOR, Manuel. *Regiões culturais do Brasil*. Rio de Janeiro: Centro Brasileiro de Pesquisas Educacionais, 1960.

DINIZ, Sílvio Gabriel. "Biblioteca setecentista nas Minas Gerais." *Revista do Instituto Histórico de Minas Gerais* 6 (1959).

—— "Um livreiro em Vila Rica no meiado do seculo xviii." *Kriterion* (Belo Horizonte) 12 (1959): 180–198.

FAZENDA, José Vieira. "Antiqualhas e memorias da cidade do Rio de Janeiro." *Revista do Instituto Histórico e Geográfico Brasileiro* 86(140) (1919): 30; 88(142) (1920): 113–116; 89(143) (1921): 93(147) (1923): 343; 95(149) (1924): 249; reprinted as *Antiqualhas e memorias da cidade do Rio de Janeiro: questões e cronicas históricas*. Rio de Janeiro: Imprensa Nacional, 1921–1927.

FRIEIRO, Eduardo. *O diabo na livraria do cônego*. Belo Horizonte: Cultura Brasileira, 1945; reprinted in his *O diabo na livraria do cônego; Como era Gonzaga?; e outros temas mineiros*. Belo Horizonte: Livraria Itatiaia, 1957.

HALLEWELL, Laurence. *Books in Brazil: A History of the Publishing Trade*. Metuchen, N.J., and London: Scarecrow Press, 1982.

—— *O livro no Brasil, sua história*. Translated by Maria da Penha Villalobos . . . e Lólio Lourenço de Oliveira. São Paulo: T. A. Queiroz, 1985.

IPANEMA, Marcello, and Cybelle de Ipanema. "Subsídios para a história das livrarias." *Revista do libro* 11(32) (January/March 1967): 22–32.

—— *A tipografia na Bahia: Documentos sobre suas origens e o empresário Silva Serva*. Rio de Janeiro: Instituto de Comunicação Ipanema, 1977.

MARTINS, Wilson. *História da inteligência brasileira*.

Vol. 1: *1550–1794*. São Paulo: Editora Cultrix, 1976.

MIRANDA, Francisco Gonçalves. *Memoria histórica da Imprensa Nacional organizada de ordem do Exmo. Sr. ministro da fazenda Dr. Homem Baptista*. Rio de Janeiro: Imprensa Nacional, 1922.

MORAES, Rubens Borba Alves de. *O bibliofilo aprendiz*. 2a ed. revista e aumentada. Rio de Janeiro: Companhia Editora Nacional, 1975.

—— *Livros e bibliotecas no Brasil colonial*. Rio de Janeiro: Livros Técnicos e Científicos, 1979.

PASSOS, Alexandre [Alexandre Passos da Silva]. "Academias e sociedades literarias nos seculos xviii e xix. Sua influencia na vida cultural bahiana." In *Anais do primeiro congresso de história da Bahia*, 5 vols. Salvador: Instituto Geográfico e Histórico da Bahia, 1950–1955.

—— *A imprensa no periodo colonial*. Rio de Janeiro:

Serviço de Documentação do Ministerio da Educação e Saude, 1952.

PFROMM NETTO, Samuel, et al. *O livro na educação*. Rio de Janeiro: Primor, 1953.

RIZZINI, Carlos. *O livro, o jornal e a tipografia no Brasil, 1500–1822*. Rio de Janeiro: Livraria Kosmos, 1946.

SILVA, Maria Beatriz Nizza da. "A livraria publica da Bahia em 1818: Obras de historia." *Revista de historia* (São Paulo) 43(87) (July/September 1971): 225–239.

—— "Produção, distribução e consumo de libros e folhetos no Brasil colonial." *Revista do Instituto Histórico e Geográfico Brasileiro* 140 (314) (January/March 1977): 78–94.

TAUNAY, Afonso de Escragnolle. "*De Brasiliae rebus pluribus*: O primeiro livro impresso no Brasil." *Anais do Museu Paulista* 7 (1936): 421–474.

THE BOOK IN SPAIN AND PORTUGAL

BOHIGAS, Pedro. *El libro español*. Barcelona: Editorial Gustavo Gili, 1962.

BONNANT, Georges. "Les Libraries du Portugal au xviie siècle vues a travers leurs relations d'affaires avec leurs fournisseurs de Genève." *Arquivo de Bibliografía Portuguesa* 6 (1960): 195–200.

CHEVALIER, Maxim. *Lectura y lectores en la España del siglo xvi y xvii*. Madrid: Edición Turner, 1976.

GAMA, Angela Maria do Monte Barcelos da. "Livreiros, editores e impresores em Lisboa no seculo xviii." *Arquivo de Bibliografía Portuguesa* 13 (1967).

GESTOSO Y PÉREZ, José. *Noticias inéditas de impresores sevillanos*. Seville, 1924.

Historia de la imprenta hispana. Madrid: Editora Nacional, 1982.

LÓPEZ, François. "Un Aperçu de la librarie espagnole au milieu du xviiie siècle." *Arquivos do Centro Cultural Portugués* 20 (1984): 469–494.

MOLL, Jaime. "Problemas bibliográficos del libro del Siglo de Oro." *Boletín de la Real Academia Española* 59 (1979): 49–107.

PÉLIGRY, Christian. "Où en est l'histoire du livre en Espagne?" *Revue française d'histoire du livre* 16 (1979): 455–475.

RICO Y SINOBAS, Manuel. *El arte del libro en España*. Madrid, 1941.

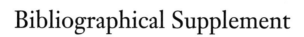

Bibliographical Supplement

PREFACE

T HIS Bibliographical Supplement to the exhibition catalogue provides full descriptions of the books and manuscripts in the exhibition catalogue, "The Book in the Americas: The Role of Books and Printing in the Development of Culture and Society in Colonial Latin America." References to published bibliographies have been provided for those seeking additional information on a particular work.

The works are arranged alphabetically by main entry: author, title, or corporate body. Reference numbers preceding the main entries link them to the exhibition catalogue. The descriptions of each printed work are governed by the *Anglo-American Cataloguing Rules* (*AACR*) and the *Bibliographic Description of Rare Books*, with some modifications in format. While the majority of these works were catalogued in adherence to *AACR* 2, a few records were done prior to the adoption of *AACR* 2, and thus follow the standards set by the first edition of the *Rules*. Most of the information presented here has also been entered into the national computerized data base known as RLIN (Research Libraries Information Network) and thus is available to RLIN subscribers nationwide.

In addition, each description contains the acquisition number and date of acquisition for the John Carter Brown Library copy. Location symbols for copies in the United States and Canada are also included, and a key to the symbols is provided at the beginning of this Bibliographical Supplement. These symbols represent libraries and institutions which have contributed cards to the *National Union Catalog, pre-1956 imprints*.

Four books were on loan from the Sutro Library for the exhibition at the John Carter Brown Library: Gabriel Biel, *Repertorium generale . . .*; Miguel de Medina, *De sacrorum hominum continentia libri V*; *Ordenanças y copilacion de leyes*; and *Decreto constitucional para la libertad de la America mexicana*. They are, respectively, items 2, 3, 5, and 28 in the main exhibition catalogue, and bibliographical data for them was kindly provided by the Sutro Library.

I would like to express my appreciation to Ilse Kramer for her advice and counsel in solving complex bibliographical problems, and to Elaine Shiner for her patience in entering these records into the RLIN data base.

SUSAN L. NEWBURY
Chief of Cataloguing

REFERENCES

ADAMS

Adams, Herbert Mayow. *Catalogue of books printed on the continent of Europe, 1501–1600, in Cambridge libraries*. London: Cambridge University Press, 1967.

ALDEN, *European Americana*

European Americana: a chronological guide to works printed in Europe relating to the Americas, 1493–1776. Ed. by John Alden with the assistance of Dennis C. Landis. New York: Readex Books, 1980–

ANDRADE, *Ensayo bib. mexicano*

Andrade, Vincente de Paula. *Ensayo bibliográfico mexicano del siglo XVII*. 2. ed. Mexico: Imprenta del Museo nacional, 1899 [i.e. 1900].

BACKER-SOMMERVOGEL

Backer, Augustine de. *Bibliothèque de la Compagnie de Jésus*. Nouv. éd. par Carlos Sommervogel. Brussels: O. Schepens; Paris: A. Picard, 1890–1932.

—— *Corrections et additions*. Par Ernest-M. Rivière. Toulouse: Rivière, 1911–1930.

BERGER, *Bib. do Rio de Janeiro*

Berger, Paolo. *Bibliografia do Rio de Janeiro de viajantes e autores estrangeiros, 1531–1900*. Rio de Janeiro: Libraria São José, 1964.

CHURCH, *Discovery*

Church, Elihu Dwight. *A catalogue of books relating to the discovery and early history of North and South America forming a part of the library of E. D. Church*. Comp. and annotated by George Watson Cole. New York: Dodd, Mead & Co.; Cambridge: University Press, 1907.

FÚRLONG CÁRDIFF, *Antonio Ruiz de Montoya*

Fúrlong Cárdiff, Guillermo. *Antonio Ruiz de Montoya y su carta a Comental, 1645*. Buenos Aires: Ediciones Theoría, 1964.

FÚRLONG CÁRDIFF, *Cartografía jesuítica del Río de la Plata*

Fúrlong Cárdiff, Guillermo. *Cartografía jesuítica del Río de la Plata*. Buenos Aires: Tallares s.a. Casa Jacobo Peuser, Itda., 1936.

GARCÍA ICAZBALCETA, *Bib. mexicana* (1954 ed.)

Garéía Icazbalceta, Joaquín. *Bibliografía mexicana del siglo XVI: catálogo razonado de libros impresos en México de 1539 a 1600*. Nueva éd., por Agustín Millares Carlo. Mexico: Fondo De Cultura Económica, 1954.

GRASES, *Historia de la imprenta en Venezuela*

Grases, Pedro. *Historia de la imprenta en Venezuela hasta el fin de la Primera República, 1812*. Caracas: Ediciones de la Presidencia de la República, 1967.

GUERRA, *Monardes*

Guerra, Francisco. *Nicolás Bautista Monardes: su vida y su obra, c. 1493–1588*. Mexico, D.F.: Compañía Fundidora de Fierro y Acero de Monterrey, 1961.

HARRISSE, *Americana*

Harrisse, Henry. *Bibliotheca Americana vetustissima; a description of works relating to America, published between the years 1492 and 1551*. New York: G. P. Philes, 1866. (Repr., Madrid: Librería General V. Suaréz, 1958.)

—— *Additions*. Paris: Tross; Leipzig: Imprimerie W. Drugulin, 1872. (Repr., Madrid: Librería General V. Suaréz, 1958.)

Historia y bib. de las primeras imprentas rioplatenses

Historia y bibliografía de las primeras imprentas rioplatenses, 1700–1850; misiones del Paraguay, Argentina, Uruguay, por Guillermo Fúrlong [et al.] Buenos Aires: Editorial Guaranía, 1953–

HUNT, *Botanical cat.*

Hunt, Rachel McMasters Miller. *Catalogue of botanical books in the collection of Rachel McMasters Miller Hunt*. Comp. by Jane Quinby. Pittsburgh: Hunt Botanical Library, 1958–1961.

J. C. BROWN, CAT., 1493–1800

Brown, John Carter. *Bibliotheca Americana: a catalogue of books relating to North and South America in the library of John Carter Brown of Providence, R.I.* Providence: Printed by H. O. Houghton & Co., Cambridge, 1865–1871.

J. C. BROWN, CAT., 1482–1700

Brown, John Carter. *Bibliotheca Americana: a catalogue of books relating to North and South America in the library of the late John Carter Brown of Providence, R.I.* Providence: Printed by H. O. Houghton & Co., Cambridge, 1875–1882.

JCB LIB., *Annual reports*

Brown University. John Carter Brown Library. *Annual reports*. Providence: The Library, 1901–1975 (Years 1901–1966, repr., with index, The Library, 1972.)

JCB LIB. CAT., PRE-1675

Brown University. John Carter Brown Library. *Bibliotheca Americana: catalogue of the John Carter Brown*

Library in Brown University, Providence, Rhode Island. 3rd ed. Providence: The Library, 1919–1931.

JONES, *Americana coll.*
Jones, Herschel Vaspasian. *Americana collection of Herschel V. Jones, a check-list (1473–1926).* Compiled by Wilberforce Eames. New York: W. E. Rudge's Sons, 1938.

LEÓN, *Bib. mexicana* (1896 ed.)
León, Nicolás. *Biblioteca mexicana. Catálogo para la venta de la porción más escogida de la biblioteca del Dr. Nicolás León.* Mexico: Impr. de "El Tiempo", 1896.

MEDINA, *Bib. hispano-americana*
Medina, José Toribio. *Biblioteca hispano-americana (1493–1810).* Santiago [Chile], 1898–1907. (Repr., Santiago [Chile], 1958–1962.)

MEDINA, *Bogotá*
Medina, José Toribio. *La imprenta en Bogotá (1739–1821).* Santiago [Chile]: Imprenta Elzeviriana, 1904. (Repr., Amsterdam: N. Israel, 1964.)

MEDINA, *Guatemala*
Medina, José Toribio. *La imprenta en Guatemala (1660–1821).* Santiago [Chile]: The author, 1910. (Repr., Amsterdam: N. Israel, 1964.)

MEDINA, *Habana*
Medina, José Toribio. *La imprenta en La Habana (1707–1810).* Santiago [Chile]: Imprenta Elzeviriana, 1904. (Repr., Amsterdam: N. Israel, 1964.)

MEDINA, *Lima*
Medina, José Toribio. *La imprenta en Lima (1584–1824).* Santiago [Chile]: The author, 1904–1907. (Repr., Amsterdam: N. Israel, 1965.)

MEDINA, *México*
Medina, José Toribio. *La imprenta en México (1539–1821).* Santiago [Chile]: The author, 1907–1912. (Repr., Amsterdam: N. Israel, 1965.)

MEDINA, *Puebla de los Angeles*
Medina, José Toribio. *La imprenta en la Puebla de los Angeles (1640–1821).* Santiago [Chile]: Imprenta Cervantes, 1908. (Repr., Amsterdam: N. Israel, 1964.)

MEDINA, *Río de la Plata*
Medina, José Toribio. *Historia y bibliografía de la imprenta en el antiguo vireinato del Río de la Plata.* La Plata: Taller de publicaciones del Museo; Buenos-Aires: F. Lajouane; London: B. Quaritch; [etc.], 1892. (Repr., Amsterdam: N. Israel, 1965.)

MEDINA, *Santiago de Chile*
Medina, José Toribio. *Bibliografía de la imprenta en Santiago de Chile desde sus orígenes hasta febrero de 1817.* Santiago [Chile]: The author, 1891.

—— *Adiciones y ampliaciones.* Santiago [Chile]: Prensas de la Universidad de Chile, 1939.

MILLARES CARLO, *Juan Pablos*
Millares Carlo, Agustín. *Juan Pablos, primer impresor que a esta tierra vino.* Mexico: Librería de M. Porrúa, 1953.

MORAES, *Bib. brasileira do período colonial*
Moraes, Rubens Borba de. *Bibliografia brasileira do período colonial.* São Paulo: Instituto de Estudos Brasileiros, 1969.

MORAES, *Bib. Brasiliana* (1983 ed.)
Moraes, Rubens Borba de. *Bibliographia Brasiliana: rare books about Brazil published from 1504 to 1900 and works by Brazilian authors of the colonial period.* Rev. and enl. ed. Los Angeles: UCLA Latin American Center Publications; Rio de Janeiro: Livraria Kosmos Editôra, 1983.

PALAU Y DULCET (2nd ed.)
Palau y Dulcet, Antonio. *Manual del librero hispano-americano; bibliografía general española e hispano-americana desde la invención de la imprenta hasta nuestros tiempos, con el valor comercial de los impresos descritos.* 2. ed. corr. y aumentada por el autor. Barcelona: A. Palau, 1948–1977.

PILLING, *Proof-sheets of a bib. of the languages of the North Amer. Indians*
Pilling, James Constantine. *Proof-sheets of a bibliography of the languages of the North American Indians.* Washington, D.C.: U.S. Government Printing Office, 1885.

SABIN
Sabin, Joseph. *Bibliotheca Americana; a dictionary of books relating to America from its discovery to the present time.* Begun by Joseph Sabin, continued by Wilberforce Eames and completed by R.W.G. Vail, for the Bibliographical Society of America. New York: Sabin, 1868–1892; Bibliographical Society of America, 1928–1936. (Repr., Amsterdam: N. Israel, 1961–1962.)

SILVA, *Diccionário bib. portuguez*
Silva, Innocêncio Francisco da. *Diccionário bibliográphico portuguez.* Lisbon: Na Imprensa nacional, 1858–1923.

SIMÓN DÍAZ, *Bib. de la lit. hispánica*
Simón Díaz, José. *Bibliografía de la literatura hispánica.* Madrid: Consejo Superior de Investigaciones Científicas, 1950–

STC
Pollard, Alfred William, and Gilbert Richard Redgrave, comps. *A short-title catalogue of books printed in England, Scotland, & Ireland and of English books*

printed abroad, 1475–1640. London: The Bibliographical Society, 1926.

STREIT, *Bib. missionum*
Streit, Robert. *Bibliotheca missionum.* Munich;
Aachen, 1916–1966.

TRELLES Y GOVÍN, *Bib. cubana de los siglos XVII y
XVIII* (2nd ed.)
Trelles y Govín, Carlos Manuel. *Bibliografía cubana
de los siglos XVII y XVIII.* 2. ed. Havana: Impr. del
Ejército, 1927.

VALLE CABRAL, *Rio de Janeiro*
Valle Cabral, Alfredo. *Annaes da Imprensa nacional
do Rio de Janeiro de 1808 a 1822.* Rio de Janeiro:
Typographia nacional, 1881.

VIÑAZA, *Bib. española de lenguas indígenas de Amér.*
Viñaza, Cipriano Muñoz y Manzano. *Bibliografía
española de lenguas indígenas de América.* Madrid:
Sucesores de Rivadeneyra, 1892.

VINDEL, *Manual*
Vindel, Francisco. *Manual gráfico-descriptivo del bib-
liófilo hispano-americano (1475–1850).* Madrid [etc.],
1930–1931.
—— *Suplemento.* 1934–

WAGNER, *Bib. mexicana*
Wagner, Henry Raup. *Nueva bibliografía mexicana
del siglo XVI, suplemento a las bibliografías de don Joaquín García Icazbalceta, don José Toribio Medina y don
Nicolás León.* Mexico: Editorial Polis, 1940 [i.e.
1946].

WAGNER, *Spanish Southwest*
Wagner, Henry Raup. *The Spanish Southwest, 1542–
1794: an annotated bibliography.* Albuquerque: The
Quivera Society, 1937.

KEY TO LOCATION SYMBOLS

CALIFORNIA

c-s   California State Library, Sutro Branch, San Francisco.

ccc   Honnold Library, Claremont Colleges.

ccamarsj   St. John's Seminary, Camarillo.

clsu   University of Southern California, Los Angeles.

clu-c   University of California at Los Angeles, William Andrews Clark Memorial Library.

csmh   Henry E. Huntington Library, San Marino.

cst   Stanford University Libraries, Stanford.

cu   University of California, Berkeley.

cu-a   University of California, Davis.

cu-b   University of California, Bancroft Library, Berkeley.

COLORADO

cₒu   University of Colorado, Boulder.

CONNECTICUT

ctht   Trinity College, Hartford.

cty   Yale University, New Haven.

cty-d   Yale University, Divinity School Library.

DISTRICT OF COLUMBIA

dc   U.S. Department of Commerce Library.

dcu   Catholic University of America Library.

ddo   Dumbarton Oaks Research Library of Harvard University.

dfₒ   Folger Shakespeare Library.

di   U.S. Department of the Interior Library.

dlc   U.S. Library of Congress.

dnlm   U.S. National Library of Medicine.

dpu   Pan American Union Library.

FLORIDA

ftasu   Florida State University, Tallahassee.

ILLINOIS

icj   John Crerar Library, Chicago.

icn   Newberry Library, Chicago.

icu   University of Chicago, Chicago.

icarbs   Southern Illinois University, Carbondale.

ien   Northwestern University, Evanston.

iu   University of Illinois, Urbana.

INDIANA

inu   Indiana University, Bloomington.

IOWA

iau   State University of Iowa, Iowa City.

KENTUCKY

kyu   University of Kentucky, Lexington.

LOUISIANA

lnht   Tulane University Library, New Orleans.

MARYLAND

mdbj   Johns Hopkins University, Baltimore.

mdbp   Peabody Institute, Baltimore.

MASSACHUSETTS

mb   Boston Public Library.

mbat   Boston Athenaeum, Boston.

mbu   Boston University.

mh   Harvard University, Cambridge.

mh-a   Harvard University, Arnold Arboretum.

mhi   Massachusetts Historical Society, Boston.

mu   University of Massachusetts, Amherst.

mwa   American Antiquarian Society, Worcester.

mwiw-c   Williams College, Williamstown, Chapin Library.

MICHIGAN

mid   Detroit Public Library.

miu   University of Michigan, Ann Arbor.

miu-c   University of Michigan, William L. Clements Library.

MINNESOTA

MnU   University of Minnesota, Minneapolis.

MISSISSIPPI

MsU   University of Mississippi, University.

MISSOURI

MoSB   Missouri Botanical Garden, St. Louis.
MoSU   St. Louis University, St. Louis.

NEW JERSEY

NjP   Princeton University, Princeton.

NEW MEXICO

NmU   University of New Mexico, Albuquerque.

NEW YORK

NBu   Buffalo and Erie County Public Library, Buffalo.
NBuU   State University of New York at Buffalo.
NHi   New York Historical Society, New York.
NIC   Cornell University, Ithaca.
NN   New York Public Library.
NNBG   New York Botanical Garden, Bronx Park, New York.
NNC   Columbia University, New York.
NNH   Hispanic Society of America, New York.
NNNAM   New York Academy of Medicine, New York.
NNUT   Union Theological Seminary, New York.
NPV   Vassar College, Poughkeepsie.

NORTH CAROLINA

NcA-S   Sondley Reference Library, Asheville.
NcD   Duke University, Durham.
NcU   University of North Carolina, Chapel Hill.

OHIO

OC   Public Library of Cincinnati and Hamilton County, Cincinnati
OCU   University of Cincinnati, Cincinnati.
OCl   Cleveland Public Library.
ODW   Ohio Wesleyan University, Delaware.
OO   Oberlin College, Oberlin.
OU   Ohio State University, Columbus.

OKLAHOMA

OkU   University of Oklahoma, Norman.

PENNSYLVANIA

PBL   Lehigh University, Bethlehem.
PHi   Historical Society of Pennsylvania, Philadelphia.
PP   Free Library of Philadelphia.
PPAN   Academy of Natural Sciences, Philadelphia.
PPC   College of Physicians of Philadelphia.
PPL   Library Company of Philadelphia.
PPRF   Rosenbach Foundation, Philadelphia.
PPT   Temple University, Philadelphia.
PPULC   Union Library Catalogue of Pennsylvania, Philadelphia.
PU   University of Pennsylvania, Philadelphia.
PV   Villanova College, Villanova.

RHODE ISLAND

RPAB   Annmary Brown Memorial Library, Providence.
RPB   Brown University, Providence.
RPJCB   John Carter Brown Library, Providence.

SOUTH CAROLINA

ScU   University of South Carolina, Columbia.

TENNESSEE

TU   University of Tennessee, Knoxville.

TEXAS

TxFTC   Texas Christian University, Fort Worth.
TxU   University of Texas, Austin.

UTAH

UU   University of Utah, Salt Lake City.

VIRGINIA

ViU   University of Virginia, Charlottesville.

WASHINGTON

Wa   Washington State Library, Olympia.
WaPS   Washington State University, Pullman.
WaU   University of Washington, Seattle.

WISCONSIN

WHi   State Historical Society of Wisconsin, Madison.

WU   University of Wisconsin, Madison.

CANADA

CaBVaU   University of British Columbia Library, Vancouver.

CaBViPA Provincial Archives, Victoria.

36

Acosta, José de, 1540–1600.

[De natura Novi Orbis libri duo]

Iosephi Acosta, Societatis Iesu. De natura Noui Orbis libri duo. ; et De promulgatione euangelii apud barbaros, siue De procuranda Indorum salute, libri sex.

Coloniae Agrippinae, : In officina Birckmannica, sumptibus Arnoldi Mylij., M.D.XCVI. [1596]

Collation: 16 cm. (8vo): †⁸ A–2N⁸ 2O⁴ (–2O4) (2O3ᵛ blank). [16], 581, [1] p.

Notes: Originally published in Salamanca, 1588. Title vignette: Jesuit trigram. "De procuranda salute Indorum, libri sex," p. 99–581.

References: JCB Lib. cat., pre-1675, I:339; Alden, *European Americana*, 596/1.

JCB Library copy: Acq: 01740. Acquired in 1855. Contains contemporary manuscript notes.

Copies: DLC, WU, PPULC, DFo, CtY, ViU, CtY-D, TxU, PU, DNLM, NN, RPJCB, NNH, ICN, NjP, MWA, MHi, RPB, CtHT, MiU-C, MH.

18

Alemán, Mateo, 1547–1614?

Ortografia castellana. / Por Mateo Aleman, criado de Su Majestad.

En Mexico. : En la emprenta de Ieronimo Balli. Año 1609. Por Cornelio Adriano Cesar., [1609]

Collation: 19 cm. (4to): π⁴ A–Y⁴ (Y4 blank). [8], 83, [1] leaves : port.

Notes: Title vignette: coat of arms. Errata statement on leaf [2] verso.

References: JCB Lib. cat., pre-1675, II:58; Medina, *México*, 244; Sabin, 715; Palau y Dulcet (2nd ed.) 6802.

JCB Library copy: Acq: 7693. Acquired in 1911. Bound in contemporary sheep and lacks the last leaf (blank).

Copies: DLC, NcD, ICU, RPB, TxU, NN, MiU, InU, OO, TU, PU, DPU, ICN, CtY, CU, CoU, NmU, IU, MH, RPJCB, NNH, MB, WaU, NcU, PPT.

19

Alemán, Mateo, 1547–1614?

Sucesos de D. frai Garcia Gera arcobispo de Mejico,

a cuyo cargo estuvo el govierno de la Nueva España. / Por el contador Mateo Aleman, criado del rei nuestro señor.

En Mexico. : En la enprenta de la viuda de Pedro Balli. Por C. Adriano Cesar., Año 1613.

Collation: 20 cm. (4to): π⁴ (–π4) A–H⁴ I² (–I2). [3], 33 leaves, [1] leaf of plates : port.

References: JCB Lib. cat., pre-1675, II:92; Medina, *México*, 273; Palau y Dulcet (2nd ed.) 6803.

JCB Library copy: Acq: 07028. Acquired in 1896 ?

Copies: NNH, RPJCB.

6

Alphonsus, a Vera Cruce, *padre*, ca. 1504–1584.

Dialectica resolutio : cum textu Aristotelis / edita per reuerendum Patrem Alphonsum a Vera Cruce Augustinianum. . . .

Mexici : Excudebat Ioannes Paulus Brissensis., Anno. 1554.

Collation: 31 cm. (fol.): 88, [10] leaves : ill.

Notes: Colophon: Liber hic finitus fuit . . . nonis Octobris [7 Oct.], anno . . . 1554. Errata, leaf 88. "Liber Prædicabilium" (leaves 3–25) is a translation of "Isagoge," an introduction to Aristotle's Categoriæ, written by Porphyry, and edited by Alphonsus, a Vera Cruce. "Sequitur Resolutio Libri Cathegoriarum Aristotelis per . . . Alphonsum a Vera Cruce . . . edita" (leaves 26–86 [i.e. 87]) consists of Aristotle's Categoriæ and a commentary by Alphonsus, a Vera Cruce.

References: Sabin, 98912; Medina, *México*, 23.

JCB Library copy: Acq: 29107. Acquired in 1941. Bound in contemporary vellum. This copy contains contemporary MS annotations, probably by the author. With: Recognitio, summularum / Alphonsus, a Vera Cruce. Mexico, 1554, and Phisica, speculatio / Alphonsus, a Vera Cruce. Mexico, 1557. Bound together subsequent to publication. This copy has MS note on t.p.: ab eode[m] autore nuc [*sic*] 20 edita et in aliq[ui]b[us] locis addita.

Copies: NN, RPJCB.

6

Alphonsus, a Vera Cruce, *padre*, ca. 1504–1584.

Phisica, speculatio, / ædita per r. P.F. Alphonsum a Vera Cruce, Augustiniæ familiæ prouintiale[m] . . . ; accessit co[m]pendium spheræ Ca[m]pani ad complementu[m] tractatus de cœlo.

Excudebat Mexici : Ioa[n]. Pau. Brisse[n]., Anno D[omi]nic[a]e incarnationis. 1557.

Collation: 31 cm. (fol.): [8], 380 p., 12 leaves : ill.

Notes: American references, p. 370–371. "Tractatus De Sphera [a]editus a magistro Campano" (12 leaves at end). Leaves 1–12 at end are numbered 1–7, 9–12 with a blank leaf between leaves 6 and 7. JCB Library catalogue describes a copy formerly owned by the Library, later exchanged for this copy, which represents a different state. There are several typographical variations, e.g. this copy has signature mark f incorrectly printed on p. 99, whereas the other copy has the correct signature mark g.

References: JCB Lib. cat., pre-1675, 1:199; Sabin, 98914.

JCB Library copy: Acq: 29108. Acquired in 1941. Bound, in contemporary vellum, with: Recognitio, summularum / Alphonsus, a Vera Cruce, Mexico, 1554, and Dialectica resolutio / Alphonsus, a Vera Cruce. Mexico, 1554. It contains contemporary MS annotations, probably by the author.

Copies: RPJCB, NNH.

6

ALPHONSUS, A VERA CRUCE, *padre,* ca. 1504–1584.

Recognitio, summularum reuerendi Patris Illdephonsi a Vera Cruce Augustiniani . . .

Mexici.: Excudebat Ioannes Paulus Brissensis., 1554.

Collation: 31 cm. (fol.): 88, [8] leaves : ill.

Notes: Colophon: Ad dei magni gloriam explicitum fuit opus tertio idus Iulii [13 July] anno. 1554. Errata, leaf 88.

References: Sabin, 98918; Medina, *México,* 22.

JCB Library copy: Acq: 29106. Acquired in 1941. Bound in contemporary vellum, with: Dialectica resolutio / Alphonsus, a Vera Cruce. Mexico, 1554, and Phisica, speculatio / Alphonsus, a Vera Cruce. Mexico, 1557. It contains contemporary MS annotations, probably by the author. In this copy the title leaf has been supplied from another copy.

Copies: NN, CSMH, NNH, RPJCB.

65

ARAUJO, ANTONIO DE, 1566–1632.

Catecismo Brasilico De Doutrina Christãa, Com o

Ceremonial dos Sacramentos, & mais actos Parochiaes. Composto Por Padres Doutos de Companhia de Jesus, Aperfeiçoado, & dado a luz Pelo Padre Antonio De Araujo da mesma Companhia Emendado nesta segunda impressaõ Pelo P. Bertholameu De Leam da mesma Companhia.

Lisboa. Na Officina de Miguel Deslandes M.DC. LXXXVI. Com todas as licenças necessarias.

Collation: 14 cm. (8vo): 16 p.l., 371,[9] p. illus. (Jesuit device).

Notes: Cut on t.p. First pub. Lisbon, 1618. License dated (15th p.l.[r]) 26 Oct. 1685. Errata, 15th p.l.[v]–16th p.l.[r] "Poemas Brasilicos Do Padre Christovaõ Valente": 3d p.l.–6th p.l.[v]

References: Moraes, *Bib. Brasiliana* (1983 ed.), 1:46; Backer-Sommervogel, 1:507; Viñaza, *Bib. española de lenguas indígenas de Amér.,* 217.

JCB Library copy: Acq: 28598. Acquired in 1940.

Copies: RPJCB.

20

BECERRA TANCO, LUIS, 1602–1672.

Felicidad De Mexico En El Principio, Y Milagroso Origen, que tubo el Santuario de la Virgen Maria N. Señora De Gvadalvpe, Extramuros: En la Apparicion admirable de esta Soberana Señora, y de su prodigiosa Imagen. Sacada à luz, y añadida por el Bachiller Lvis Bezerra Tanco, Presbytero, difunto; para esta segunda impression, que ha procurado el Doctor D. Antonio de Gama . . . Con Licencia.

En Mexico, por la Viuda de Bernardo Calderon Año de 1675.

Collation: 20.5 cm. (4to): 11 p.l., 31 numb. l. fold. plate.

Notes: Errata: 1.31[v]. First pub. under title: Origen milagroso del Santuario de Nuestra Señora de Guadalupe. Mexico, 1666. "Censvra" (5th p.l.) dated: Mexico, y Junio 24. de 1675. años.

References: Medina, *México,* 1121; Palau y Dulcet (2nd ed.) 26230; Andrade, *Ensayo bib. mexicano,* 663; cf. Sabin, 4216.

JCB Library copy: Acq: 04379. Acquired before 1902.

Copies: RPJCB, LNHT.

2

BIEL, GABRIEL, d. 1495.

[Super quatuor libros sententiarum (1527)]

Repertorium generale & succinctum: veru[m] tame[n] valde vtile atq[ue] necessariu[m]: contento-

ru[m] in quatuor collectorijs, acutissimi ac profundissimi theologi Gabrielis Biel super quatuor libros
sententiarum.

Impressum est hoc Egregium opus in inclita ciuita-
te Lugdun[um] per probum virum Jacobum Myt/
Sumptu notabilis viri Symonis vincentij bibliopole.
Anno a Christonato. M.cccccxxvij. [1527].

Collation: 27 cm.: Unfoliated; ca. 600 leaves.

Notes: Title in red and black. Illustrated title page
with publisher's device. Two columns to the page.
Includes indexes.

References: Adams, 1:2004.

Sutro Library copy: Acq: Purchased from Librería
Abadiano by Adolph Sutro, 1885. Branded: Sello del
Convento de Santiago [Tlatelolco]. Title page signed
by Juan de Zumárraga, Bishop of Mexico.

Copies: CLSU, C-S.

71

BRAZIL.

Decreto. Tendo-me constado, que os prélos, que se
achão nesta capital, erão os destinados para a secretaria de estado dos negocios estrangeiros, e da
guerra.

[Rio de Janeiro : Na Impressão Regia, 1811]

Collation: 29 cm. (fol.): 1 sheet (verso blank).

Notes: Issued as the 19th work in v. 1 of: Brazil.
[Laws, etc.] Codigo Brasiliense. Rio de Janeiro: Na
Impressão Regia, 1811. Title from caption and beginning of text. Dated at end: Rio de Janeiro em treze
de Maio de mil oitocentos e oito.

Copies: NN, MH, RPJCB.

67

CAMÕES, LUÍS DE, 1524?–1580.

[Lusiadas]

Os Lusiadas de Luis de Camões.

Impressos cm Lisboa, : em casa de Antonio
Go[n]çaluez impressor., 1572.

Collation: 18 cm. (4to): π² A–Y⁸ Z¹⁰. [2], 186 leaves.

Notes: In verse. This is the so-called E edition. Controversy exists over whether it really was printed in
1572 or at a much later date as a pirated edition. It
gets its name from the seventh line of the first stanza
which begins with the word "Entre." On the title
page, the pelican faces toward the reader's right.
Another edition of the same year, the so-called Ee
edition, begins the seventh line of the first stanza "E

entre." On the title page, the pelican faces the reader's
left. Title within border. Discusses Vasco de Gama's
1st voyage to India and mentions Mexico and Brazil.

References: Alden, *European Americana*, A572/2; Silva,
Diccionário bib. portuguez, V:250.

JCB Library copy: Acq: 68–511. Acquired in 1968.

Copies: MH, NNH, RPJCB.

44

CARRIÓ DE LA VANDERA, ALONSO, b. ca. 1706.

El Lazarillo De Ciegos Caminantes desde Buenos-
Ayres, hasta Lima con sus Itineratios segun la mas
puntual observacion, con algunas noticias utiles á los
Nuevos Comerciantes que tratan en Mulas; y otras
Historicas. Sacado De Las Memorias Que hizo Don
Alonso Carriò de la Vandera en este dilatado Viage,
y Comision que tubo por la Corte para el arreglo de
Correos, y Estafetas, Situacion, y ajuste de Postas,
desde Montevideo. Por Don Calixto Bustamente
Carlos Inca, alias Concolorcorvo Natural del Cuzco,
que acompañó al referido Comisionado en dicho
Viage, y escribiò sus Extractos.

Con Licencia. En Gijon, en la Imprenta de la Rovada.
Año de 1773. [i.e., Lima, 1775 or 1776]

Collation: 15.5 cm. (8vo): 246 l. fold. table.

Note: Authorship and date: cf. Alonso Carrió de la
Vandera, *Itineraire de Buenos-Aires à Lima* . . . Paris,
1961 [i.e. 1962], p. [1]–17.

References: J. C. Brown, Cat., 1493–1800, III:1856;
Sabin, 9566; Medina, *Lima*, 1354; Palau y Dulcet (2nd
ed.) 37707.

JCB Library copy: Acq: 04201. Acquired in 1869.
Bound in contemporary vellum.

Copies: DLC, MnU, CU, NCD, CtY, RPJCB, InU.

7

CASAS, BARTOLOMÉ DE LAS, 1474–1566.

[Brevissima relacion]

Breuissima relacion de la destruycion de las Indias : /
colegida por el obispo do[n] Fray Bartolome de las
Casas, o Casaus de la Orden de Sa[n]cto Domingo.,
Año. 1552.

Fue impressa . . . enla . . . ciudad de Seuilla : en casa
de Sabastian Trugillo . . . a Nuestra Señora de Gracia.,
Año de. M.D.Lij. [1552, i.e. 1553]

Collation: 20 cm. (4to): a–e⁸ f¹⁰ g⁴ (f10ᵛ blank). [108]
p.

Notes: Publication statement from colophon: leaf
f10ʳ. Church indicates that these nine tracts constitute

a collection for which bibliographers have determined no particular arrangement. The individual works, printed between 1552 and 1553, are also found bound separately. The complete set could not have been issued before 1553. The pagination and signatures given are for the "Brevissima relacion" and for "Lo que se sigue es un pedaço de una carta y relacion" which is appended to it. The pagination and signatures for the other works in this issue are found as part of their analytical cataloging records. Title and coat of arms within woodcut border.

Partial contents: "Aqui se contiene una disputa, o controversia . . . ," Seville : Sebastian Trugillo, 1552., [124] p. — "Aqui se contienen treynta proposiciones muy juridicas . . . ," Seville : Sebastian Trugillo, 1552., [20] p. — "Este es un tratado . . . ," Seville : Sebastian Trugillo, 1552., [72] p. — "Entre los remedios . . . ," Seville : Jacome Cromberger, 1552., [108] p. — "Aqui se contienen unos avisos y reglas . . . ," Seville : Sebastian Trugillo, 1552., [32] p. — "Tratado comprobatorio del Imperio sobrano . . . ," Seville : Sebastian Trugillo, 1553., [160] p. — "Principia quedam ex quibus procedendum est in disputatione . . . ," Seville : Sebastian Trugillo, [1553 ?], [20] p.

References: JCB Lib. cat., pre-1675, 1:167; Alden, *European Americana,* 552/8; Church, *Discovery,* 87.

JCB Library copy: Acq: 0252. Acquired in 1846. Contemporary marginal manuscript notes with some partially lost due to trimming; gathering a is bound out of order; several manuscript texts bound in at the end.

Copies: NjP, InU, MB, MH, MWiW-C, CtY, OCl, LNHT, ViU, RPJCB, CU-B, MBAt, NN, CSmH, DLC, PPULC, NNH, MiU-C, PPRF, FTaSU.

8

CASAS, BARTOLOMÉ DE LAS, 1474–1566.

[Brevissima relacion. Latin]

Narratio regionum indicarum per Hispanos quosdam deuastatarum verissima : / priùs quidem per Episcopum Bartholemæum Casaum, natione Hispanum Hispanicè conscripta, & anno 1551. Hispali, Hispanicè anno verò hoc 1598. Latinè excusa.

Francofurti, : sumptibus Theodori de Bry, & Ioannis Saurii typis., Anno M.D. XCVIII. [1598]

Collation: 21 cm. (4to):):(4 A–R4 S4 (–S4). [8], 141, [1] p. : ill.

Notes: Translation of: Tyrannies et cruautez des Espagnols. Antwerp : F. Raphelengius, 1579; itself a translation of: Brevissima relacion. Seville : Sebastian Trugillo, 1552. Engraved title page.

References: JCB Lib. cat., pre-1675, 1:360; Alden, *European Americana,* 598/20.

JCB Library copy: Acq: 0683. Acquired in 1846.

Copies: ViU, RPJCB, NcA-S, MiD, DLC, PPULC, MiU-C, NN, MB, OCl, MWiW-C, PBL, PPL.

27

CATHOLIC CHURCH.

[Liturgy (Mozarabic rite)]

Missa Gothica seù Mozarabica, et officium itidèm Gothicum, diligentèr ac dilucidè explanata ad usum percelebris Mozárabum sacelli Toleti á munificentissimo Cardinali Ximenio erecti; et in obsequium illmi. perindè ac venerab. d. decani et capituli sanctae ecclesiae Toletanae, Hispaniarum et Indiarum primátis.

Angelopoli [Puebla, Mexico] : Typis Seminarii Palafoxiani, Anno Domini M.DCC.LXX. [1770]

Collation: 30 cm. (fol.): ¶4 A–2K2 2L4 (–2L4) 2A–3D2 (–3D2). [8], 137, [1], 198 p. : ill., music.

Notes: Edited by Francisco Antonio Lorenzana and Francisco Fabian y Fuero; cf. p. [7]. Page 133, 2nd count, misnumbered 233. Each of the 3 full-size engravings appears to have been pasted to a preceding blank leaf. Therefore they have been collated as part of a gathering rather than as leaves of plates.

References: Sabin, 49459; Medina, *Puebla de los Angeles,* 864; Palau y Dulcet (2nd ed.) 172923.

JCB Library copy: Acq: 9261. Acquired in 1913. Bound in contemporary sheep.

Copies: DLC, CtY, NN, CU-B, MBU, MB, CCamarSJ, ICN, MiU-C, RPJCB.

10

CATHOLIC CHURCH.

[Testerian catechism]

[18th century]

Collation: 16 cm. : [13] leaves, bound.

Notes: MS. European paper, watermarked. Date of MS based on León's pamphlet; cf. León, Nicolás. *Un catecismo mazahua (en jeroglífico testeramerindiano).* Mexico, 1968, p. 19. This MS contains [13] leaves. The last one, however, is blank, as is the verso of the next to the last one and the recto of the first one.

Contents: Todo fiel christiano; Pater noster; Ave Maria; Credo; Salve Regina; Decalogue; Commandments; Sacraments; Articles of Religion; Works of Mercy; Confession; Declarations of the "Nombres señal del cristiano" of the Creed, the Decalogue, and the Sacraments — all in questions and answers.

References: Glass, J. B. "Census of Middle Amer. Testerian manuscripts" (In: *The Handbook of Middle Amer. Indians*, v. 14, article 25, no. 826).

JCB Library copy: Acq: 69–109. Acquired in 1968. Bound in contemporary tanned crushed hide.

Copies: RPJCB.

34

CATHOLIC CHURCH. Province of Lima. Concilio Provincial (1583).

Tercero cathecismo y exposicion de la doctrina christiana, por sermones. : Para que los curas y otros ministros prediquen y enseñen a los Yndios y a las demas personas. / Conforme alo que en el sancto Concilio Prouincial de Lima se proueyo.

Impresso . . . en la Ciudad delos Reyes [Lima], : por Antonio Ricardo . . . , Año de M.D.LXXXV. [1585]

Collation: 22 cm. (4to): ¶⁸ 2A–3D⁸ (–3D8) (2B3, 2G3, 2K5 missigned 2A3, HG3, 2K6). Leaf 2N6 is a cancel. Some copies do not contain this cancel. [8], 215 leaves.

Notes: Sommervogel attributes authorship to José de Acosta and Juan de Atienza. Cf. Medina. Numerous errors in pagination. Jesuit trigram on title page. Errata statement: leaf [1] verso. Includes index.

References: JCB Lib. cat., pre-1675, 1:303; Sabin, 94838; Medina, *Lima*, 3.

JCB Library copy: Acq (copy 1): 10353. Acquired in 1914. Acq (copy 2): 01671. Acquired in 1853. (1) with: Doctrina Christiana / Concilio Provincial. Lima, 1584. Lacks leaves [8] and 73. Signature of Joseph de Acosta on title page. (2) bound separately without the cancel. Preliminaries bound in different order than that given in Medina. On title page with signature of Joseph de Acosta: Concuerda con el original.

Copies: NN, DLC, RPJCB.

32

CIEZA DE LEÓN, PEDRO DE, 1518–1560.

[La chronica del Peru. Part 1]

Parte Primera Dela chronica del Peru. Que tracta la demarcacion de sus prouincias: la descripcion dellas. Las fundaciones de las nuevas ciudades. Los ritòs y costumbres de los indios. Y otras cosas estrañas dignas de ser sabidas. Fecha por Pedro d' Cieza de Leon vezino de Seuilla. 1553. Con priuillegio Real.

Impressa en Seuilla en casa de Martin de montesdoca.

Acabose a quinze de Março de mill y quinientos y cinquenta y tres años.

Collation: 28 cm. (fol.): 10 p.l., cxxxiiii numb. l. : ill.

Notes: Title in red and black. Cut (royal arms) on t.p. Imprint at end. Errata, 10th p.l.ᵛ. License dated (2d p.l.ʳ) 14 Sept. 1552. The "Chronica" left by Cieza de Leon was divided into four parts. Only the first part was published before the 19th century.

References: JCB Lib. cat., pre-1675, 1:175; Sabin, 13044; Medina, *Bib. hispano-americana*, 157; Palau y Dulcet (2nd ed.) 54646; Streit, *Bib. missionum*, II:644.

JCB Library copy: Acq: 0840. Acquired before 1866. Part of the margin of the t.p. is wanting; restored in pen and ink facsim.

Copies: DLC, ICN, RPJCB, NNH, NN, ViU.

12

CIUDAD REAL, ANTONIO DE, 1551–1617.

[Maya-Spanish and Spanish-Maya dictionary: the Diccionario de Motul]

[After 1577: probably ca. 1600–1630]

Collation: 16 cm. (v.1), 17 cm. (v.2): 2v., bound; v.1: 214, [1], 215–465 leaves; v.2: 83, [3], 105–160, 162–170, 175–208, 217–232, 234–236 leaves.

Notes: MS, in various hands. Vol. 1 without distinguishable watermark; v.2 with watermark of crowned circles. Vol. 1 prepared after 1577, the date cited on leaf 58 verso, line 5, where the author mentions a comet which he saw in that year. Vol. 2 is the work of a later copyist, probably written in an early 17th-century hand. Authorship based on Cogolludo's chronicle of Yucatan in which he distinguished Antonio de Ciudad Real's two-volume bilingual dictionary, such as this is, from his six-volume Calepino; cf. López Cogolludo, D., *Historia de Yucathan*, Madrid, 1688.

Contents: Vol. 1 contains alphabetical entries of Maya words, their Spanish equivalents, explanations in Spanish of Maya usage, and, in places, fuller descriptions of plants, animals, customs, etc. in Yucatan; v.2 contains alphabetical entries of Spanish words with Maya equivalents.

References: J. C. Brown Cat., 1482–1700, 1:556; Cf. Pilling, *Proof-sheets of a bib. of the languages of the North Amer. Indians*, 806.

JCB Library copy: Acq: 02673. Acquired in 1854. V.2 has portions wanting between leaves [1] and 105, 160 and 162, 170 and 175, 208 and 217, and 232 and 234. Laid in to v.2 are 6 MS leaves which contain texts of sermons in Maya.

Copies: RPJCB.

60

Compañía de María Santísima de la Enseñanza de México.

Relacion historica de la fundacion de este Convento de Nuestra Señora del Pilar, Compañia de Maria, llamada vulgarmente la enseñanza, en esta ciudad de México, y compendio de la vida y virtudes de N.M.R.M. Maria Ignacia Azlor y Echeverz su fundadora y patrona. . . .

En México : Por don Felipe de Zúñiga y Ontiveros, calle del Espiritu Santo, Año de 1793.

Collation: 21 cm. (4to): 1–22⁴ 23². [10], ii, 165, [3] p., [1] leaf of plates : port.

References: Sabin, 69226; Medina, *México*, 8255; Palau y Dulcet (2nd ed.) 259736.

JCB Library copy: Acq: 04288. Acquired in 1872. Bound in contemporary sheep.

Copies: DLC, PBL, NN, RPJCB.

26

CORTÉS, HERNÁN, 1485–1547.

[Cartas. Carta 2a–4a]

Historia de Nueva-España, / escrita por su esclarecido conquistador Hernan Cortes, ; aumentada con otros documentos, y notas, por el ilustrissimo señor don Francisco Antonio Lorenzana, . . .

En México : en la imprenta del Superior Gobierno, del Br. D. Joseph Antonio de Hogal en la Calle de Tiburcio., Año de 1770.

Collation: 28 cm. (fol.): π² ¶–3¶² χ1 A² ¶–4 ¶² B–5N² 5O² (–5O2) (π1ᵛ and π2ᵛ blank). [22], XVI, 400, [18] p., 4 leaves of plates; [1] leaf, 32 [i.e. 31] leaves of plates : ill., maps, plan.

Notes: The 2nd, 3rd, and 4th letters of Cortes with notes and additional material by Lorenzana. Title vignette: allegorical figures with motto: Opibus clara, religione nobilior. Between pages 176 and 177 are inserted the [1] leaf and [31] leaves of plates. Leaf [1] recto is a printed title: Cordillera de los pueblos . . . Leaf [1] verso, blank. The 31 leaves of plates are illustrative of a Mexican codex, the first 13 plates unnumbered, the remaining 18 plates numbered 15–32. Errata statement: χ1ʳ (1st alphabet).

References: Medina, *México*, 5380; Wagner, *Spanish Southwest*, 152; Sabin, 16938.

JCB Library copy: Acq: 05741. Acquired before 1874.

Copies: SCU, CTY, WAPS, VIU, NCU, MHI, WHI, OC, INU, CABVIPA, RPJCB, CU, PBL, NN, MWA, PP, MNU,

MIU-C, CSMH, IU, MDBP, NJP, DLC, MSU, FTASU, OCL, LNHT, MB, NCD, IAU, NNH, PPL.

25

[COYOACÁN CODEX. Pictorial codex in the Nahuatl language]

[ca. 1700 to before 1743]

Collation: 25 cm.: [14] leaves : ill.

Notes: One of a group of colonial Mexican MSS known as "Techialoyan Codices." On native "amatl" paper made from fig tree bark. Deals with landholdings near the town of Coyoacán, a town in the valley of Mexico. Date of MS based on Robertson's article; cf. Robertson, Donald. "Techialoyan manuscripts and paintings, with a catalog". (In : *The Handbook of Middle American Indians*, v. 14, article 24, no. 713).

JCB Library copy: Acq: 29022. Acquired in 1941. First and last leaves glued to modern paper. Some leaves are faded and illegible.

Copies: RPJCB.

66

CUNHA, LUIS ANTÓNIO ROSADO DA.

Relaçaõ da entrada que fez o excellentissimo, e reverendissimo senhor D. Fr. Antonio do Desterro Malheyro bispo do Rio de Janeiro, em o primeiro dia deste prezente anno de 1747. havendo sido seis annos bispo do reyno de Angola, donde por nomiaçaõ [*sic*] de Sua Magestade, e bulla pontificia, foy promovido para esta diocesi. / Composta pelo doutor Luiz Antonio Rosado de Cunha juiz de fóra, e provedor dos defuntos, e auzentes, capellas, e residuos do Rio de Janeiro.

Rio de Janeiro : Na segunda officina de Antonio Isidoro de Fonceca., Anno de M.CC.XLVII. [1247, i.e. 1747]

Collation: 20 cm. (4to): [A]¹² (A12 blank). 20, [4] p.

Note: The first book printed in Brazil; cf. Moraes, *Bib. Brasiliana*.

References: Moraes, *Bib. Brasiliana* (1983 ed.), I:239; Moraes, *Bib. brasileira do periodo colonial*, 112.

JCB Library copy: Acq: 74–197. Acquired in 1974.

Copies: NN, RPJCB.

39

ERCILLA Y ZÚÑIGA, ALONSO DE, 1533–1594.

[Araucana]

Primera, segunda, y tercera partes de la Araucana de don Alonso de Ercilla y Çuñiga . . .

En Madrid, : En casa de Pedro Madrigal., Año de 1590.

Collation: 15 cm. (8vo): §–4§⁸ A–3D⁸ (3D2 +χ1) 3E–3K⁸ (2D4 blank). [32], 394, [1], 395–436, [12] leaves : port.

Notes: Narrative poem on Spanish efforts to subdue Araucanian Indians. The earliest edition to incorporate all 3 pts.; pt. 1 1st published: Madrid, 1569, pt. 2 1st published: 1578 and pt. 3 1st published: Madrid, 1589. Errata, leaf [3] verso, 1st count. "Segunda parte de la Araucana" (leaves [197]–365) and "Tercera parte de la Araucana" (leaves [366]–436) have special title pages which are dated 1589. Includes index.

References: JCB Lib. cat., pre-1675, 1:322; Alden, *European Americana,* 590/24.

JCB Library copy: Acq: 02571. Acquired about 1851.

Copies: NHi, RPJCB, CtY.

57

FIDALGO DELVAS.

[Relaçam verdadeira]

Relaçam verdadeira dos trabalhos q[ue] ho gouernador do[m] Ferna[n]do d[e] Souto [e] certos fidalgos portugueses passarom no d[e]scobrime[n]to da prouincia da Frolida [*sic*]. / Agora nouame[n]te feita per hu[m] fidalgo Deluas.

[Evora] : Foy impressa . . . em casa de Andree de Burgos . . . acabouse aos dez dias de febreiro do anno de mil [e] quinhentos [e] cincoenta [e] sete annos. na nobre [e] sempre leal cidade de Euora., [1557]

Collation: 14 cm. (8vo): a–y⁸ z⁴. clxxx leaves.

Note: Imprint taken from colophon.

References: Alden, *European Americana,* 577/33.

JCB Library copy: Acq: 30690. Acquired in 1950.

Copies: NN, RPJCB.

70

GAMA, JOSÉ BASILIO DA, 1740–1795.

O Uraguay : poema / de José Basilio da Gama na Arcadia de Roma Termindo Sipilio.

Lisboa : Na Regia officina typografica, Anno MDCCLXIX [1769]

Collation: 16 cm. (8vo): [A]–G⁸ (–G8). [6], 102, [2] p.

Note: Title vignette: royal arms of Portugal.

References: Sabin, 26487; Moraes, *Bib. Brasiliana* (1983 ed.), 1:338; Palau y Dulcet (2nd ed.) 97316.

JCB Library copy: Acq: 63–171. Acquired in 1963.

Copies: NN, ICN, MH, RPJCB.

53

GARRIGA, ANTONIO, 1662–1733.

Instruccion practica para ordenar santamente la vidà; que ofrece el P. Antonio Garriga de la Compania de Iesus. Como brebe memorial, y recuerdo à los que hazen los exercicios espirituales de S. Ignacio de Loyola fundador de la misma Compañia.

En Loreto [Paraguay], : con licencia de los superiores en la imprenta de la Compañia, Año de 1713.

Collation: 14 cm. (8vo): [2], 120 p.

Note: Leaves unsigned.

References: Historia y bib. de las primeras imprentas rioplatenses, 5; Palau y Dulcet (2nd ed.) 100285.

JCB Library copy: Acq: 5527. Acquired in 1909.

Copies: RPJCB.

4

GERSON, JEAN, 1363–1429.

[Opusculum tripartitum. Spanish]

Tripartito del christianissimo y consolatorio doctor Juan Gerson de doctrina christiana : a qualquiera muy p[ro]uechosa. / Traduzido de latin en le[n]gua castellana para el bie[n] d[e] muchos necessario.

Impresso en Mexico : En casa de Juan Cromberger. Por ma[n]dado y a costa del. R.S. obispo de la mesma ciudad fray Jua[n] Çumarraga. Reuisto y examinado por su mandado., Año de. M.d. xliiij. [1544]

Collation: 21 cm. (4to): a–c⁸ d⁴. [56] p. : ill.

Notes: Translation of: Opusculum tripartitum, itself 1st published: Cologne, ca. 1467. Title within illustrated border.

References: JCB Lib cat., pre-1675, 1:137; Sabin, 27168; Medina, *México,* 6; Harrisse, *Americana,* 250; Church, *Discovery,* 82.

JCB Library copy: Acq: 07502. Acquired in 1896.

Copies: DLC, RPJCB, NN, CtY, CSmH, RPAB.

11

GILBERTI, MATURINO, 1498–1585.

Dialogo de doctrina christiana, enla lengua d[e] Mechuaca[n]. / Hecho y copilado de muchos libros de sana doctrina, por el muy reuerendo padre fray Maturina Gylberti dela orden del seraphico padre sant Fra[n]cisco. ; Trata delo que ha de saber creer, hazer, dessear, y aborrecer, el christiano. Va preguntando el discipulo al maestro. = Y yeti siranda y qui aringahaca dialogo aringani, ychuhca hi[m?]bo chupengahaqui christianoengani, yngui vca tata che[n?] casireq[ua?] fray Maturino Gilberti sant Fra[n]cisco tata. Teparimento am baqueti. Ma hurengua reri curamarihati tepari hurendahperini. Ca hurendaperi mayocucupanstahati hurenda eq[ua?] embani.

[Mexico City] : Fue impresso en casa de Juan Pablos Bressano . . . desta . . . ciudad de Mexico., Año de. 1559.

Collation: 30 cm. (fol.): a⁴ b–z⁸ &⁸ 2a–2q⁸ 2r⁴. ccxcv, 25 leaves.

Notes: Place of publication and printer's name taken from colophon. Title within illustrated border. Numerous errors in foliation.

References: JCB Lib. cat., pre-1675, I:204; Medina, *México*, 36; Sabin, 27358; Palau y Dulcet (2nd ed.) 102196; Viñaza, *Bib. española de lenguas indígenas de Amér.*, 27; Millares Carlo, *Juan Pablos*, 33.

JCB Library copy: Acq: 06680. Acquired in 1896. Contains two copies of the title page both of which are damaged. Gathering 2k is misbound between gatherings 2l and 2m.

Copies: NN, RPJCB, NNH, CSmH, ICN.

69

GONZAGA, TOMÁS ANTÔNIO, 1744–1807?

[Marilia de Dirceo]

Marilia de Dirceo. / Por T.A.G. ; Parte I [–III]. Nova edicção.

Lisboa : na typografia Lacerdina., 1819–[1820]

Collation: 14 cm. (12mo): A–I¹² K1–5+. 280 p.

Notes: In verse. Parts 2 and 3 have half titles only which read: Marilia de Dirceo. Parte II [–III]. Part 1 originally published: Lisbon, 1792; pt. 2 originally published: Lisbon, 1799; pt. 3 originally published: Lisbon, 1800. Although pt. 3 has no indication of place, printer, or date, Borba de Moraes believes that it was printed in 1820; cf. Moraes, *Bib. Brasiliana* (1983 ed.), 1:364. Errata statement on p. 226.

References: Moraes, *Bib. Brasiliana* (1983 ed.), 1:364.

JCB Library copy: Acq: 74–247. Acquired in 1974. Lacks part 3. The description of this part is based on Borba de Moraes. This copy is bound in contemporary calf.

Copies: DLC, ICN, MH, RPJCB, DCU.

72

GUIMARÃES, MANUEL FERREIRA DE ARAUJO, 1777–1838.

Elementos de astronomia par uso dos alumnos da Academia Real Militar / ordenado [*sic*] por Manoel Ferreira de Araujo Guimarães sargento mór do Real Corpo de Engenheiros, e lente do quarto anno da referida Academia.

Rio de Janeiro. : Na Impressam Regia., Anno M.DCC.XIV [i.e. 1814].

Collation: 21 cm. (4to): π⁴ 1–35⁴ (354 blank). [8], 178 [i.e. 278], [2] p., iv folded leaves of plates : ill.

Notes: Date of publication based on Valle Cabral. Title vignette: royal arms of Portugal. Pages 263, 273 and 278 misnumbered 253, 278, and 178 respectively. Errata statement on p. [5–7].

References: Valle Cabral, *Rio de Janeiro*, 352.

JCB Library copy: Acq: 73–101. Acquired in 1973. Bound in contemporary sheep.

Copies: RPJCB.

17

HERNÁNDEZ, FRANCISCO, 1514–1587.

[Rerum medicarum Novae Hispaniae thesaurus. Spanish]

Quatro libros. De la naturaleza, y virtudes de las plantas, y animales que estan receuidos en el vso de medicina en la Nueua España, y la methodo, y correccion, y preparacion, que para administrallas se requiere con lo que el doctor Francisco Hernandez escriuio en lengua latina. : Muy vtil para todo genero de gente q[ue] viue en esta[n]cias y pueblos, de no ay medicos, ni botica. / Traduzido, y aumentados muchos simples, y compuestos y otros muchos secretos curatiuos, por Fr. Francisco Ximenez, hijo del conuento de S. Domingo de Mexico, natural de la villa de Luna del reyno de Aragon.

En Mexico, : En casa de la viuda de Diego Lopez Daualos. 1615 Vende[n]se en la tienda de Diego Garrido, en la esquina de la calle de Tacuba, y en la porteria de S. Domingo., [1615]

Collation: 20 cm. (4to): 2¶⁴ A–3D⁴ 3E². [5], 23, 23–150, 161–203, [7] leaves : ill.

Notes: Leaves 5, 7 misnumbered 4, 6 respectively. Translation of: Rerum medicarum Novae Hispaniae Thesaurus; seu, Plantarum, animalium, mineralium Mexicanorum historia. Title vignette; title within ornamental border. Errata statement at end. Includes index.

References: JCB Lib. cat., pre-1675, II:108; Sabin, 31514; Medina, *México*, 297; Hunt, *Botanical cat.*, 200.

JCB Library copy: Acq: 01822. Acquired in 1851.

Copies: RPJCB, MB, NNH, CSt, InU, MH, PPC, MWiW-C, MiU-C, CSmH, NN.

64

JESUITS.

[Correspondence from the East]

Auisi particolari delle Indie di Portugallo riceuuti in questi doi anni del .1551. & 1552. da li reuere[n]di padri de la co[m]pagnia de Iesu, doue fra molte cose mirabili, si uede delli paesi, del le genti, & costumi loro & la grande co[n]uersioue [*sic*] di molti populi, che cominciano a riceuere il lume della sa[n]ta fede & relligione [*sic*] christiana.

In Roma : Per Valerio Dorico, & Luigi fratelli Bressani alle spese de M. Batista di Rosi genouese., 1552.

Collation: 16 cm. (8vo): A–C⁸ D⁴ E–K⁸ L⁴ M⁸ N⁴ O⁸ P⁴ (–P4) Q–S⁸ T⁶ (F8, G8, P3 blank; P2 missigned P3). 85, [3], 86–99, [2], 100–169, 180–200, 200–208, [2], 209–267, [1] p.

Notes: Some copies also issued with a second part continuing the pagination to p. 316; cf. Alden. Title vignette: Jesuit trigram. Numerous errors in pagination. Errata statement at end.

References: JCB Lib. cat., pre-1675, 1:166; Cf. Alden, *European Americana*, 552/28.

JCB Library copy: Acq: 03734. Acquired in 1867. Lacks leaves F8, G8, and P3 (all blanks).

Copies: RPJCB.

24

JUANA INÉS DE LA CRUZ, *sister*, 1648–1695.

Carta Athenagorica De La Madre Jvana Ynes De La Crvz Religiosa Profesa De Velo, y Choro en el muy Religioso Convento de San Geronimo de la Ciudad de Mexico cabeça. de la Nueba España. Qve Imprime, Y Dedica A La Misma Sor, Phylotea De La Crvz [pseud.] Su estudiosa aficionada en al Convento de la Santissima Trinidad de la Puebla de los Angeles.

Con licencia en la Puebla de los Angeles en la Imprenta de Diego Fernandez de Leon. Año de 1690. Hallarase este papel en la libreria de Diego Fernandez de Leon debajo de el Portal de las Flores.

Collation: 20 cm. (4to): 18 l.

Notes: Occasioned by "vn Sermon del Mandato, que predicò el Reverendissimo P. Antonio de Vieyra de la Compañia de Jesus, en el Colegio de Lisboa." License dated (1st p.l.ᵛ) 25 Nov. 1690. Phylothea de la Cruz

is the pseudonym of Manual Fernández de Santa Cruz y Sahagún.

References: Palau y Dulcet (2nd ed.) 65265; Medina, *Puebla de los Angeles*, 131; Backer-Sommervogel, VIII: 661.

JCB Library copy: Acq: 1048. Acquired in 1905.

Copies: RPJCB, CU-B, NNH, InU.

23

JUANA INÉS DE LA CRUZ, *sister*, 1648–1695.

Villancicos, Que Se Cantaron En La Santa Iglesia Cathedral de Mexico, à los Maytines del Gloriosissimo Principe de la Iglesia, el Señor San Pedro. . . . Año de 1677. . . .

Con Licencia. En Mexico, por la Uiuda de Bernardo Calderon. [1677]

Collation: 20 cm. (4to): 4 l.

Notes: Caption title; imprint from verso of l. 4. Woodcut title vignette (bust of St. Peter). Text begins: Señor mio, ofrezcole à V. Señoria, . . .

References: Medina, *México*, 1157.

JCB Library copy: Acq: 28932. Acquired in 1941. Bound, in contemporary vellum, as no. 32 with 42 other items.

Copies: RPJCB.

21

KINO, EUSEBIO FRANCISCO, 1644–1711.

Exposicion Astronomica De El Cometa, Que el Año de 1680. por los meses de Noviembre, y Diziembre, y este Año de 1681. por los meses de Enero y Febrero, se ha visto en todo el mundo, y le ha observado en la Ciudad de Cadiz, El P. Eusebio Francisco Kino De la Compañia de Jesvs.

Con Licencia, en Mexico por Francisco Rodriguez Lupercio. 1681.

Collation: 20 cm. (22 cm. in case): 8 p.l., 28 numb. l. ill., fold. chart.

Notes: Cut (Virgin Mary) on t.p. Licenses (5th – 6th p.l.) dated 24 Sept 1681. A reply to: Sigüenza y Góngora, Carlos de, Manifiesto philosóphico contra los cometas, Mexico, 1681.

References: Palau y Dulcet (2nd ed.) 128015; Medina, *México*, 1228; Backer-Sommervogel, IV:1044; Sabin, 37936.

JCB Library copy: Acq: 05742. Acquired in 1909. Bound in contemporary vellum.

Copies: MiU-C, TˣU, CSmH, RPJCB.

29

LOBO, MANUEL, 1612–1686.

Relacion de la vida, y virtudes del V. hermano Pedro de San Ioseph Betancur. De la Tercera orden de penitencia de N. Seraphico P.S. Francisco. Primer fundador del hispital [*sic*] de convalencientes de N. Señora de Belen, en la ciudad de Guatemala. / Por el P. Manuel Lobo de la Compañia de Iesus.

Con licencia, impressa en Guatemala, : Por Ioseph de Pineda Ybarra, Año de 1667.

Collation: 16 cm. (8vo): π^2 ¶^{8} χ1 A–T^4 V^2 (D2 missigned C2). [11], 76, [2] leaves.

References: Cf. JCB Lib. cat., pre-1675, III:161; Sabin, 41712; Medina, *Guatemala*, 20; Palau y Dulcet (2nd ed.) 139500; Streit, *Bib. missionum*, II:2003; Backer-Sommervogel, IV:1894.

JCB Library copy: Acq: 84–22. Acquired in 1984. Bound in contemporary goat.

Copies: RPJCB.

73

LUCCOCK, JOHN.

Notes on Rio de Janeiro, and the southern parts of Brazil; taken during a residence of ten years in that country, from 1808–1818. / By John Luccock.

London : Printed for Samuel Leigh, in the Strand., MDCCCXX. [1820]

Collation: 29 cm.: π^4 χ^4 A–4G^4 4H–4P^2 (L2 missigned K2). xv, [1], 639, [1] p., [3] leaves of plates (2 folded) : maps, plan.

Notes: Erratum on p. [1], 1st count. Bookseller's advertisement at end. "A glossary of those Tupi words, which occur in the preceding pages," p. [629]–639.

References: Sabin, 42620; Moraes, *Bib. Brasiliana* (1983 ed.), I:500; Berger, *Bib. do Rio de Janeiro*, 191.

JCB Library copy: Acq: 06176. Acquired before 1844. The map of the table land of Brazil misbound facing the title page. This copy contains numerous contemporary manuscript notes including 2 pages of them bound in following the title page.

Copies: NjP, ViU, MU, MWA, RPJCB, MdBP, PPL, ODW, MiU-C, NN, MB, DLC, NBuU, FTaSU, NBu, ICarbS, CU, UU, OU.

60 : FIGURE 78

Mapa del Presidio de San Antonio de Bexar, i sus Misiones de la Provinsia de Texas Fhô en 24, del Mes de Marzo de 1764. Por el Capitan Don Luis Anttonio Menchaca que lo es de Dhô Presidio. [1764].

Notes: MS map, in ink on paper: 36.7 x 47 cm.

References: JCB Lib. *Annual reports*, 13:25, 40:23–24.

JCB Library copy: Acq: 5788. Acquired in 1909.

Copies: RPJCB.

61

MASÚSTEGUI, PEDRO.

Arte de construccion: / por el M.R.P.M. fray Pedro Masustegui, difinidor, y procurador general de la provincia de predicadores de San Antonino del nuevo reyno de Granada.

Con licencia en Sta. Fé [de Bogotá] : Por D. Antonio Espinosa., Año de 1784.

Collation: 16 cm. (8vo): A–M^8 N^4 (–N4) (N3^v blank). 197, [1] p.

Notes: Originally published: Seville, 1734; cf. Palau y Dulcet. Title within ornamental border. Page 121 is misnumbered 221.

References: Medina, *Bogotá*, 11; Palau y Dulcet (2nd ed.) 157625n.

JCB Library copy: Acq: 9631. Acquired in 1913–1914. Bound in contemporary vellum.

Copies: NN, RPJCB, CtY, NBuU.

3

MEDINA, MIGUEL DE, 1489–1578.

De sacrorum hominum continentia libri V. : In quibus sacri & ecclesiastici caelibatus origo, progresio, & consummatio ex sancta scriptura, sanctorumq[ue], patrum scriptis proponitur, statuitur, & ab haereticorum nostri temporis calumnijs propugnatur, & defenditur. / F. Michaele Medina Hispano.

Venitiis : Ex officina Iordani Zileti, 1569.

Collation: 32 cm.: 20 leaves, 539 p.

Notes: Two columns to the page. Includes index. Printer's device on title page.

References: Palau y Dulcet (2nd ed.) 159658; Simón Díaz, *Bib. de la lit. hispánica*, XIV:3970.

Sutro Library copy: Acq: Purchased from Librería Abadiano by Adolph Sutro, 1885. Branded: Sello del Convento de Santiago [Tlatelolco]. Title page signed by Fray Juan Baptista.

Copies: NNUT, DCU, C-S.

45

Mercurio peruano de historia, literatura, y noticias públicas que da à luz la Sociedad academica de amantes de Lima. Y en su nombre D. Jacinto Calero y Moreira. — Tomo I. Enero . . . 1791 — Tomo XII. [1794]

Impreso en Lima : En la imprenta real de los Niños Huérfanos., [1791] – 1795.

Collation: 22 cm. (4to): 12 v. : ill., map.

Contents: Vol. 1: nos. 1–34, Jan. 2, 1791 – Apr. 28, 1791; v.2: nos. 35–68, May 1, 1791 – Aug. 28, 1791; v.3: nos. 69–103, Sept. 1, 1791 – Dec. 29, 1791; v.4: nos. 104–138, Jan. 1, 1792 – Apr. 29, 1792; v.5: nos. 139–173; May 3, 1792 – Aug. 30, 1792; v.6: nos. 174–208, Sept. 2, 1792 – Dec. 30, 1792; v.7: nos. 209–242, Jan. 3, 1793 – Apr. 28, 1793; v.8: nos. 243–278, May 2, 1793 – Aug. 31, 1793; v.9: nos. 279–312, Sept. 5, 1793 – Dec. 29, 1793; v.10: nos. 313–346, Jan. 2, 1794 – Apr. 27, 1794; v.11: nos. 347–382, May 1, 1794 – Aug. 31, 1794; v.12: nos. 583–611 [i.e. 383–411], 1794.

Notes: Publication statement for vols. 2, 5–11 reads: En Lima: en la imprenta real de los Niños Expósitos. The map is in v. 3, the illustrations in vols. 9 & 11, and there are folded tables in several vols. Errata statements appear in several of the vols.

References: J. C. Brown Cat., 1493–1800, III:3475; Sabin, 47935; Streit, *Bib. missionum*, III:1152; Medina, *Lima*, 1744.

JCB Library copies: Acq: (copy 1): 09780, 09781. Acquired before 1882. Acq: (copy 2): 09861. Acquired after 1882. Vols. 1–12 as well as a second copy of v. 11. Vol. 11, copy 1 has p. 170 misnumbered 160 and the index is bound at the end. Vol. 11, copy 2 is bound in contemporary vellum, has p. 170 correctly numbered, is wanting the plate, and has the index bound after the title page. Vol. 12 has duplicates of p. 189–190.

Copies: N ͨU, NN, MB, PU, DLC, T ˣU, InU, IU, RPJCB, LNHT, ICN, PPL, OU.

28

MEXICO.

[Constitución de Apatzingán]

Decreto Constitucional para la Libertad de la America Mexicana : sancionado en Apatzingan á 22 de octubre de 1814.

[Apatzingán] : Imprenta Nacional, [1814].

Collation: 21 cm.: 34 p.

Notes: The first Mexican Constitution. Printed on the portable press of the Insurgents. Signed by José María Liceaga, José María Morelos, José María Cos, and Remigio de Yarza.

References: Palau y Dulcet (2nd ed.) 69560.

Sutro Library copy: Acq: Purchased from Librería Abadiano by Adolph Sutro, 1885.

Copies: C-S.

15

MONARDES, NICOLÁS, ca. 1512–1588.

[Dos libros. El uno trata de todas las cosas]

Dos libros. : El vno trata de todas las cosas q[ue] trae[n] de n[uest]ras Indias Occide[n]tales, que siruen al vso de medicina . . . El otro libro, trata de dos medicinas marauillosas q[ue] son co[n]tra todo veneno . . . con la cura delos venenados. . . . / Agora nueuamente co[m]puestos por el doctor Niculoso de Monardes medico de Seuilla.

Seuilla : en casa de Sabastian Trugillo., Acabose a diez y seys dias del mes de Iunio., 1565.

Collation: 15 cm. (8vo): a–q⁸ r⁴ (r4ᵛ blank). [264] p.

Notes: Place of publication, printer, and date of publication (except for the year) from colophon (p. [261]) Includes index.

References: Alden, *European Americana*, 565/45; Guerra, *Monardes*, 7.

JCB Library copy: Acq: 15555. Acquired in 1929. Bound in contemporary calf. In this copy, the title page border is hand-colored. Also in this copy, the number "51" in manuscript appears on the title page before the word "marauedis."

Copies: NN, RPJCB, DNLM.

16

MONARDES, NICOLÁS, ca. 1512–1588.

[Primera y segunda y tercera partes de la historia medicinal. English]

Ioyfull nevves out of the newe founde worlde, : wherein is declared the rare and singular vertues of diuerse and sundrie hearbes, trees, oyles, plantes and stones, with their aplications, as well for phisicke as chirurgerie . . . / Englished by Jhon Frampton marchaunt.

Imprinted at London : in Poules churche-yarde, by Willyam Norton., Anno Domini. 1577.

Collation: 19 cm. (4to): *⁴ (–*4) A–2D⁴ 2E². [3], 109, [1] leaves : ill.

Notes: "The Seconde Part Of This Booke Is Of The Things that are brought from our Occidentall Indias . . . Made by the Doctor Monardus" (leaves 33–86) and "The Third Parte Of The Medicinall Historie" (leaves 87–109) have special half titles. There is another issue with title : The three bookes written in the Spanish tongue. London, 1577. These are the same sheets with cancel title page.

References: JCB Lib. cat., pre-1675, 1:266; Alden, *European Americana*, 577/33; STC 18005a; Guerra, *Monardes*, 19.

JCB Library copy: Acq:01798. Acquired in 1854. The last leaf is misbound preceding leaf 1.

Copies: MB, MdBJ, DLC, ICN, OkU, CaBVaU, RPJCB, NjP, CtY, WU, NN.

46

El Monitor araucano periodical ministerial y politico. — [Tom. 1], no. 1 (6 Abr. 1813) — Tom. 2, [no. 84] (1 Oct. 1814).

Santiago de Chile : En la imprenta de gobierno P.D.J.C. Gallardo., 1813–1814.

Collation: 22 cm. (4to): 2 v.

Notes: Edited by Camilo Henríquez. Published every Tuesday, Thursday, and Saturday from Apr. 6 – Dec. 4th, 1813; published every Tuesday and Friday from Dec. 7, 1813 – Oct. 1, 1814; with extra numbers published at irregular intervals. Publication statements vary on some issues.

References: Medina, *Santiago de Chile*, 64.

JCB Library copy: Acq: 85-175. Acquired in 1985. Contains the following issues: v.1, nos. 3, 9, 17, 22, 30; v.2, no. 82. Description of the entire serial is based on information taken from Medina.

Copies: DLC, LNHT, CU, RPJCB.

5

NEW SPAIN.

[Laws, etc.]

Con preuilegio. Ordena[n]ças y copilacion de leyes: hechas por el muy illustre señor don Antonio d[e] Me[n]doça Visorey y Gouernador desta Nueua España : y Preside[n]te de la Audie[n]cia Real q[ue] en ella reside : y por los Señores Oydores d[e] la dicha audie[n]cia : p[ar]a la bue[n]a gouernacio[n] y estilo d[e] los oficiales della. Año d[e] M. D. xlviij.

A gloria y honrra de nuestro señor Jesu xpo aqui se acaban las Ordena[n]ças [y] copilacion de leyes nueuame[n]te ordenadas y copiladas por el muy Illustre señor do[n] Antonio d[e] Me[n]doça Visorrey y Gouernador desta nueua españa; y Preside[n]te de la audie[n]cia Real q[ue] en ella reside : y por los Señores Oydores : p[ar]a la buena gouernacio[n] y estilo d[e] los oficiales d[e]lla. Y fuero[n] por su ma[n]do impressas e[n] la muy leal y gra[n] ciudad d[e] Mexico e[n] casa d[e] Jua[n] pablos : acabaro[n]se d[e] imp[ri]mir a. xxij. dias d[e]l mes d[e] marçço d[e] M. d. xlvijj [1548] años.

Collation: 31 cm.: xlv leaves.

Notes: Folio XLiiij misnumbered XLV. Title page in red and black, with ornamental borders and coat of arms of Emperor Charles V. First book of laws printed in the Americas.

References: García Icazbalceta, *Bib. mexicana* (1954 ed.), 16; Medina, *México*, 14; Wagner, *Bib. mexicana*, 16; Palau y Dulcet (2nd ed.) 163666.

Sutro Library copy: Acq: Purchased from Libreria Abadiano by Adolph Sutro, 1885. Royal letter of approval and index pages mutilated.

Copies: NN, C-S.

17 : FIGURES 21–24

NIEREMBERG, JUAN EUSEBIO, 1595–1658.

Ioannis Eusebii Nierembergii Madritensis ex Societate Iesu ... historia naturæ, maxime peregrinæ, libris XVI. distincta. In quibus rarissima naturæ arcana, etiam astronomica, & ignota Indiarum animalia ... plantæ, metalla, lapides ... fluuiorumáue & elementorum conditiones, etiam cum proprietatibus medicinalibus, describuntur ... : Accedunt de miris & miraculosis naturis in Europâ libri duo: item de iisdem in terrâ Hebræis promissâ liber vnus.

Antverpiæ, : ex officina Plantiniana Balthasaris Moreti., M. DC. XXXV. [1635]

Collation: 34 cm. (fol.): *4 A–3D6 3E4 (*1v, 3E4 blank). [8], 502, [106] p. : ill.

Notes: Title vignette: printer's device. Includes index.

References: JCB Lib. cat., pre-1675, II:258; Alden, *European Americana*, 635/94.

JCB Library copy: Acq: 0379. Acquired in 1846.

Copies: MiU, MB, MnU, RPJCB, MH-A, DDO, MoSU, OCU, InU, NNBG, NcU, NIC, MdBP, PV, DFo, PU, CLU-C, NNNAM, DLC, CtY, DNLM, ScU, WU, NPV, OU, MoSB, IaU.

31

Noticia del establecimiento del museo de esta capital de la Nueva Guatemala. Y exercicios publicos de historia natural que han tenido en la sala de estudios de dicho museo. Los bachilleres en filosofia don Pascasio Ortiz de Letona, cursante en leyes, y don Mariano Antonio de Larrabe en medicina. Bajo la direccion de don Jose Longinos Martinez, naturalista de la real expedicion facultativa de este reyno, y Nueva España, profesor de botanica &c. Con motivo de la aperatura del Gavinete de historia natural, que en celebridad de los años de nuestra augusta reyna y señora, le dedicò, ofreciò, y consagrò dicho naturalista, en su dia 9. de diciembre de 1796.

[Guatemala] : Impreso en la oficina de la viuda de D. Sebastian de Arevalo, Año de 1797.

Collation: 21 cm. (4to): [A]–C⁴ χ² (χ1ᵛ, χ2 blank). [2], 23, [3] p.

Note: Place of publication based on Medina.

References: Medina, *Guatemala*, 909; Palau y Dulcet (2nd ed.) 193480.

JCB Library copy: Acq: 86–20. Acquired in 1986. Bound in contemporary paper wrappers.

Copies: RPJCB.

56

NÚÑEZ CABEZA DE VACA, ALVAR, 16th cent.

[Relación y comentarios]

La relacion que dio Aluar Nuñez Cabeça de Vaca de lo acaescido en las Indias en la armada donde yua por gouernador Pa[m]philo de Narbaez, desde el año de veynte y siete hasta el año d[e] treynta y seys que boluio a Seuilla con tres de su compañia.

Fue impresso . . . en . . . Zamora : Por . . . Augustin de Paz y Juan Picardo . . . A costa y espensas del virtuoso varon Juan Pedro Musetti . . . de Medina del Campo., [6 Oct. 1542].

Collation: 21 cm. (4to): A–H⁸ I⁴ (–I4) (I3ᵛ blank). [134] p.

Notes: Imprint from colophon which is dated: Acabose en seys dias del mes de octubre. Año del nasçimiento d[e] n[uest]ro Saluador Jesu Cristo de mil y quinientos y quarenta y dos años. Title vignette: coat of arms.

References: Alden, *European Americana*, 542/21.

JCB Library copy: Acq: 15554. Acquired in 1929. Bound in contemporary vellum and lacks p. [13–14] which have been replaced in facsim.

Copies: NN, RPJCB, TˣFTC.

40

OÑA, PEDRO DE, 1570?–1643?

[Arauco domado]

Primera parte de Arauco domado, / compuesto por el licenciado Pedro de Oña. . . .

Impresso en la Ciudad delos Reyes [Lima], : Por Antonio Ricardo de Turin. . . . , Año de 1596.

Collation: 21 cm. (4to): ¶¹² A–X⁸ X⁴ Y–2T⁸ 2V⁴. [12], 70, 70–77, 76–139 [i.e., 133], 133–164, [4], 165–335, [1] leaves : port.

Notes: In verse. No more published. Errata statement on leaf [2] verso, 1st count.

References: JCB Lib. cat., pre-1675, I:347–348; Sabin, 57300; Medina, *Lima*, 10.

JCB Library copy: Acq: 0678. Acquired in 1846. Lacks leaf [12], 1st count; available in facsim.

Copies: NN, NNH, RPJCB, INU, MB.

41

OÑA, PEDRO DE, 1570?–1643?

Temblor de Lima año de 1609. . . . y vna cancion real panegyrica . . . / por el licenciado Pedro de Oña.

En Lima : Por Francisco del Canto., 1609.

Collation: 21 cm. (4to) : A–C⁸ (–C8). 23 leaves.

Notes: In verse. Place of publication from colophon. Title vignette: coat of arms.

References: JCB Lib. cat., pre-1675, II:65; Medina, *Lima*, 42.

JCB Library copy: Acq: 0692. Acquired in 1846.

Copies: RPJCB.

62

PARRA, ANTONIO.

Descripcion de diferentes piezas de historia natural las mas del ramo maritimo, : representadas en setenta y cinco laminas. / Su autor don Antonio Parra.

En la Havana : Año de 1787. En la imprenta de la Capitanía General., [1787]

Collation: 21 cm. (4to): π⁴ a–i⁴ j–z⁴ χ⁶ (–χ6) (π4ᵛ, χ5ᵛ blank).

Notes: Page 99 misnumbered 69. Errata statement at end. Includes indexes.

References: Medina, *Habana*, 90; Sabin, 58835; Palau y Dulcet (2nd ed.) 213307; Trelles y Govin, *Bib. cubana de los siglos XVII y XVIII* (2nd ed.), 149.

JCB Library copy: Acq: 8108. Acquired in 1911. Bound in contemporary sheep.

Copies: DI, CtY, INU, NN, NIC, PPAN, RPJCB, MiU.

37

PERU (Viceroyalty)—Laws, statutes, etc., 1590–1596 (Hurtado de Mendoza) 21 July 1594.

Ordencas [sic] Qve El Señor Marqves De Cañete Visorey De estos Reynos del piru mando hazer para el remedio de los excessos, que los Corregidores de Naturales hazen en tratar, y contratar con los Indios, y daños, y agrauios, que de esto reciben. Con Otras Cosas Enderecadas [sic] Al bien y conseruacion de los dichos Indios.

Impresso en la Ciudad de los Reyes [Lima], con licencia de su Excelencia, por Antonio Ricardo de Turin [1594].

Collation: 28 cm. (fol.): [7] p.

Notes: Caption title; imprint at end. Dated p. [7] "en la ciudad de los Reyes" 21 July 1594.

References: JCB Lib. cat., pre-1675, 1:333; Medina, *Lima,* 8.

JCB Library copy: Acq: 06887. Acquired in 1888. Bound as the 2d of 3 items with: Silva, Juan de. Advertencias importantes, Madrid, 1621.

Copies: RPJCB.

68

PIMENTA, MIGUEL DÍAS, ca. 1661–1715.

Noticias Do Que He O Achaque Do Bicho, Diffiniçam Do Seu crestamēto, subimento corrupçaõ, sinaes, & cura atè, o quinto grao, ou intensaõ delle, suas differenças, & cõplicaçoẽs, com que se ajunta. Por Miguel Dias Pimenta, Familiar do S. Officio, & residente no Arrecife de Pernambuco.

Lisboa. Na Officina de Miguel Manescal, Impressor do Santo Officio. Anno de 1707

Collation: 14.5 cm. (8vo): 4 p.l., 175, [1] p.

Note: License dated (last page) 18 July 1703.

References: Moraes, *Bib. Brasiliana* (1983 ed.), II :670; Silva, *Diccionário bib. portuguez,* VI :235.

JCB Library copy: Acq: 32790. Acquired in 1960. Bound in contemporary vellum.

Copies: RPJCB.

54 : FIGURE 73

QUIROGA, JOSÉ, 1707–1784.

Mapa de las Missiones de la Compañia de Jesvs en los rios Paranà y Vruguay; conforme àlas mas modernas observaciones de Latitud, y de Longitud, hechas en los pueblos de dichas Missiones, y à las relaciones antiguas, y modernas de los Padres Missioneros de ambos rios. Por el Padre Joseph Quiroga de la misma Compañia de Jesus en la Provincia de el Paraguay. Año de 1749.

Ferdinandus Franceschelli sculp. Romae an. 1753.

Notes: Engraved map, 4 sheets joined, 38″ x 31¾″. Dedication to Ferdinand VI, king of Spain.

References: Fúrlong Cárdiff, *Cartografía jesuítica del Río de la Plata,* 32.

JCB Library copy: Acq: C–6708. Acquired in 1966–1967.

Copies: RPJCB.

52

RUIZ DE MONTOYA, ANTONIO, 1585–1652.

[Arte]

Arte de la lengua guarani / por el p. Antonio Ruiz de Montoya de la Compañia de Jesus ; con los escolios anotaciones y apendices del p. Paulo Restivo de la misma compañia sacados de los papeles del p. Simon Bandini y de otros.

En el pueblo de S. Maria la Mayor. [Paraguay] : [s.n.], El año de el Señor MDCCXXIV. [1724]

Collation: 21 cm. (4to): π² A–Q⁴ R² 2A–2O⁴ 2P² 2Q–3I⁴ 3K². [4], 132, 256 p.

Notes: Text in Spanish and Guarani. Originally published as part of: Arte, y bocabulario de la lengua guarani / Antonio Ruiz de Montoya. Madrid: Juan Sanchez, 1640. "Supplemento" (p. 1–256), edited by Paolo Restivo, contains appendices and "Particulas de la lengua guarani" (p. 117–256).

References: Sabin, 74033; Viñaza, *Bib. española de lenguas indígenas de Amér.,* 282; Streit, *Bib. missionum,* II :1670n; Fúrlong Cárdiff, *Antonio Ruiz de Montoya,* 34n.

JCB Library copy: Acq: 06288. Acquired before 1900.

Copies: TXU, INU, RPJCB.

50

RUIZ DE MONTOYA, ANTONIO, 1585–1652.

[Arte]

Arte, y bocabulario de la lengua guarani. / Compuesto por el padre Antonio Ruiz, de la Compañia de Iesus.

En Madrid : por Iuan Sanchez., Año 1640.

Collation: 19 cm. (4to): ¶⁶ A–3A⁴ a–c⁴ d–q⁸ r² (r2 blank). [12], 376, 234, [2] p.

Notes: The Guarani grammar (p. 1–100) has caption title: Arte de la lengua guarani; the Spanish-Guarani vocabulary (p. 101–376, 1–234) has caption title: Vocabulario de la lengua guarani. Parte primera. Ruiz de Montoya's Guarani-Spanish vocabulary was published in the previous year, with title: Tesoro de la lengua guarani. Title vignette: portrait of the Virgin Mary with the legend: Sanabiles fecit nationes orbis terrarum Sap. cap. 1, and surrounded by the words: Concebida sin mancha de pecado original. Errata statement on p. [4–5].

References: Alden, *European Americana*, 640/164; Fúrlong Cárdiff, *Antonio Ruiz de Montoya*, 34.

JCB Library copy: Acq: 28600. Acquired in 1940. Lacks last leaf (blank).

Copies: NN, RPJCB, ViU.

49

RUIZ DE MONTOYA, ANTONIO, 1585–1652.
[Catecismo]

Catecismo de la lengua guarani, / compuesto por el padre Antonio Ruyz de Compañia de Iesus.

En Madrid, : por Diego Diaz de la Carrera, año M. DC. XXXX. [1640]

Collation: 15 cm. (8vo): π⁸ A–X⁸. [16], 336 p.

Notes: Text in Guarani and Spanish in parallel columns. Title vignette: Jesuit trigram. Numerous errors in pagination. Errata statement on p. [3].

References: Alden, *European Americana*, 640/165; Fúrlong Cárdiff, *Antonio Ruiz de Montoya*, 33.

JCB Library copy: Acq: 28599. Acquired in 1940.

Copies: NN, NNH, RPJCB.

48

RUIZ DE MONTOYA, ANTONIO, 1585–1652.

Señor. Antonio Ruiz de Montoya de la Compañia de Iesus, y su procurador general de la prouincia del Paraguay, dize: que estando prohibido por cedulas, y ordenes reales, so graues penas, que los portugueses del Brasil no puedan entrar en la dicha prouincia .

[Madrid : s.n., 1639 or 1640]

Collation: 31 cm. (fol.): π². [4] p.

Notes: Title from caption and beginning of text. Publication statement taken from Fúrlong Cárdiff.

References: JCB Lib. cat., pre-1675, II:88; Alden, *European Americana*, 639/102; Fúrlong Cárdiff, *Antonio Ruiz de Montoya*, 27.

JCB Library copy: Acq: 03811. Acquired in 1868.

Copies: RPJCB.

51

RUIZ DE MONTOYA, ANTONIO, 1585–1652.
[Vocabulario]

Vocabulario de la lengua guarani / compuesto por el padre Antonio Ruiz de la Compañia de Iesus ; revisto, y augmentado por otro religioso de la misma compañia.

En el pueblo de S. Maria la Mayor. [Paraguay] : [s.n.], El año de MDCCXXII. [1722]

Collation: 22 cm. (4to): [4], 168, 162–327, [2], 328–589 p.

Notes: Spanish-Guarani vocabulary. Edited by Paolo Restivo, the "otro religioso de la misma compañia". Originally published as part of: Arte, y bocabulario de la lengua guarani / Antonio Ruiz de Montoya. Madrid: Juan Sanchez, 1640. In this edition the leaves are unsigned; there is a blank leaf between p. 327 and 328.

References: Sabin, 74032; Viñaza, *Bib. española de lenguas indígenas de Amér.*, 278; Streit, *Bib. missionum*, II:1670n; Fúrlong Cárdiff, *Antonio Ruiz de Montoya*, 34n.

JCB Library copy: Acq: 28425. Acquired in 1939. Pages 137–144 are repeated between the blank leaf and p. 328.

Copies: RPJCB.

30

SÁENZ OVECURI, DIEGO.

Thomasiada al sol de la iglesia, y su doctor santo Thomas de Aquino. / Por el padre fray Diego Saenz Ovecuri, de la orden de predicadores, maestro de estudiantes, y aora lector de theologia, presentado en ella, y vicario provincial.

Impressa en Guatemala, : Por Ioseph de Pineda Ybarra, impressor de libros, Año de 1667.

Collation: 22 cm. (4to): ¶–3¶⁴ §–4§⁴ *4 A–3C⁴ (3C3ᵛ, 3C4 blank). [32], 161, [35] leaves, [1] folded leaf of plates : ill., coat of arms.

Notes: In verse. Errata statement at end. Includes index.

References: Sabin, 74852; Medina, *Guatemala*, 22; Palau y Dulcet (2nd ed.) 284383.

JCB Library copy: Acq: 62-41. Acquired in 1962. Bound in contemporary vellum, and lacks the folded table.

Copies: InU, RPJCB.

13

SAHAGÚN, BERNARDINO DE, d. 1590.

Psalmodia christiana, y sermonario de los sanctos del año, en lengua mexicana: / co[m]puesta por el muy.

R. padre fray Bernardino de Sahagun, de la orden de sant Francisco. ; Ordenada en cantares ò psalmos: paraque canten los indios en los areytos, que hazen en las iglesias.

En Mexico. : Con licencia, en casa de Pedro Ocharte., M.D.LXXXIII. años. [1583]

Collation: 20 cm. (4to): π^4 A–Z^8 &^{8} 2A–2E^8 2F^4 (E2 missigned A2). [4], 236 leaves : ill.

Notes: Psalms are written in Nahuatl. Title vignette: depiction of Christ on the Cross. Errors in foliation.

References: JCB Lib. cat., pre-1675, 1:298; Sabin, 74935; Medina, *México*, 98; Palau y Dulcet (2nd ed.) 284991; Viñaza, *Bib. española de lenguas indígenas de Amér.*, 75.

JCB Library copy: Acq: 799. Acquired in 1905. Bound in contemporary vellum and contains contemporary manuscript notes.

Copies: NN, RPJCB, CSMH.

55

SAN ALBERTO, JOSÉ ANTONIO DE, 1727–1804.

Carta circular, ò edicto, de el ilustrisimo, y reverendisimo señor D. Fr. Josef Antonio de S. Alberto, del Consejo de S.M. y obispo de Cordova del Tucuman: dirigida a todos sus amados hijos, y diocesanos, que desean, y solicìtan, y que en adelante solicitaren ser promovidos à los sagrados ordenes.

Buenos Ayres. : MDCCLXXXI. En la real Imprenta de los Niños Expositos., [1781].

Collation: 21 cm. (4to): A–N^4. [2], 102 p.

Notes: Title vignette. Bookseller's advertisement at end of title page.

References: Sabin, 75971; Medina, *Río de la Plata*, 12; *Historia y bib. de las primeras imprentas rioplatenses*, 20; Palau y Dulcet (2nd ed.) 289479.

JCB Library copy: Acq: 68–310. Acquired in 1968. Bound in contemporary vellum.

Copies: CTY, RPJCB, ICN.

47

SAN MARTÍN, JOSÉ DE, 1778–1850.

Proclama a los habitantes del estado de Chile. Compatriotas: al fin se acerca el dia tan suspirados por vosotros, como por nuestros hermanos del Perú.

[Santiago, Chile : s.n., 1820]

Collation: 29 x 19 cm. (1/2º); 1 sheet (verso blank).

Notes: Title from caption and beginning of text.

Signed at end: San Martin. Dated at end: Santiago Junio 17 de 1820.

JCB Library copy: Acq: 85–176. Acquired in 1985.

Copies: RPJCB.

59

SIGÜENZA Y GÓNGORA, CARLOS DE, 1645–1700.

Descripcion, Que De La Vaia de Santa Maria de Galve (antes Pansacola) de la Movila, y Rio de la Paliçada, en la Costa Septentrional del seno Mexicano, hizo Don Carlos de Siguença y Gongora, Cosmographo del Rey nuestro Señor, y Cathedratico Jubilado de las Ciencias Mathematicas, en la Academia Mexicana, yendo para ello en compañia de Don Andrès de Pes, Cavallero de la Orden de Santiago, Almirante de la Real Armada de Barlovento, à cuyo cargo iba la Fragata Nuestra Señora de Guadalupe, y la Valandra San Joseph, por orden del Excelentissimo señor Conde de Galve, Virrey, Governador, y Capitan General de la Nueva España, Año de 1693.

[Madrid? ca. 1720]

Collation: 30.5 cm. (31.5 cm. in case). (fol.): 16 numb. l.

Notes: Caption title. Dated (l. 16^r): A bordo de la Fragata Nuestra Señora de Guadalupe, surta en el Puerto de San Juan de Ulua, à 15. de Mayo de 1693. años.

References: Wagner, *Spanish Southwest*, 62b; Jones, *Americana coll.*, 406.

JCB Library copy: Acq: 28582. Acquired in 1940.

Copies: RPJCB.

22

SIGÜENZA Y GÓNGORA, CARLOS DE, 1645–1700.

Libra Astronomica, Y Philosophica En Que D. Carlos de Siguenza y Gongora Cosmographo, y Mathematico Regio en la Academia Mexicana, Examina no solo lo que à su Manifiesto Philosophico contra los Cometas opuso el R. P. Eusebio Francisco Kino de la Compañia de Jesus; sino lo que el mismo R.P. opinò, y pretendio haver demostrado en su Exposicion Astronomica del Cometa del año de 1681. Sacala à luz D. Sebastian De Gvzman Y Cordova . . .

En Mexico: por los Herederos de la Viuda de Bernardo Calderon IXI. DC. XC. [1690]

Collation: 20.5 cm. (22.5 cm. in case). (4to): 12 p.l., 188 p. tables, diagrs.

Notes: Cut (winged horse) on t.p. "Prologo" dated (p.l. 11) 1 Jan 1690. Dedication (p.l. 3–7) by Sebastian

Guzman y Córdova. A reply to: Kino, E. F. *Exposición astronómica*, Mexico, 1681, and Torre, Martin de la. *Manifiesto cristiano en favor de los cometas*, Mexico, 1681. Includes (p. 8–19) his Manifiesto philosóphico contra los cometas, 1st pub. Mexico, 1681.

References: Palau y Dulcet (2nd ed.) 312974; Medina, *México*, 1484; Sabin, 80976; Wagner, *Spanish Southwest*, 62a.

JCB Library copy: Acq: 28581. Acquired in 1940.

Copies: NN, RPJCB, ICJ, CSMH, NNH, CU-B, CtY, InU, CU-B.

9

SPAIN.

[Laws, etc.]

Leyes y ordenanças nueuame[n]te hechas por Su Magestad, p[ar]a la gouernacion de las Indias y buen tratamiento y conseruacion de los indios: que se han de guardar en el consejo y audie[n]cias reales q[ue] en ellas residen: y por todos los otros gouernadores, juezes y personas particulares dellas.

Fueron impressas . . . en la villa de Alcala de Henares : En casa de Joan de Brocar, A ocho dias del mes de julio del año de n[uest]ro saluador Jesu Christo. M.D.XLIII [8 July 1543]

Collation: 30 cm. (fol.): A¹⁰ B⁴ (–B4). xiij leaves.

Notes: Publication statement taken from colophon. There is another issue printed on vellum which has slight typographical differences; cf. Church. Title page illustrated with large woodcut of the royal arms of Spain.

References: JCB Lib. cat., pre-1675, 1:135; Alden, *European Americana*, 543/18; Church, *Discovery*, 80; Palau y Dulcet (2nd ed.) 137548.

JCB Library copy: Acq: 0248. Acquired in 1846.

Copies: DLC, CSMH, InU, RPJCB, NNH, NN.

33

SPAIN.

Pragmatica sobre los diez dias del año.

Impressa . . . en esta dicha Ciudad de los Reyes [Lima] . . . : por Antonio Ricardo., Año M.D.LXXXIIII. [1584]

Collation: 29 cm. (fol.): π². [4] p.

Notes: Caption title. Publication statement from colophon.

References: JCB Lib. cat., pre-1675, 1:301; Palau y Dulcet (2nd ed.) 235209.

JCB Library copy: Acq: 7471. Acquired in 1910. Con-

temporary manuscript note concerning place and date of reading of the proclamation; with: Prematica con la forma y medios de la reducion de la moneda de vellon a su justo valor / Spain. Madrid: [s.n.], 1627.

Copies: MH, RPJCB.

43

SUÁREZ DE FIGUEROA, MIGUEL.

Templo De N. Grande Patriarca San Francisco De La Provincia De los doze Apostoles de el Peru en la Ciudad de los Reyes arruinado, restaurado, y engrandecido de la providencia Divina. En Panegyrico Historial, Y poetico certamen. . . . Escrivelo Obediente Hijo De la Prouincia el P. Predicador Fr. Miguel Suarez de Figueroa.

Con licencia En Lima, Año de 1675.

Collation: 20 cm. (4to): 8 p.l., 23 numb. l., 1 l., [33] p. 4 plates (incl. 1 fold.).

Notes: Dated at end, 31 Dec. 1674. "Visita, Y Declaracion que hizo el P. Pred., Fr. Juan de Benauides . . . en la residencia del R.ᵐᵒ P.Fr. Luis Zervala. . ." : p. [1–33].

References: Palau y Dulcet (2nd ed.) 323936; Medina, *Lima*, 496; Sabin, 93319; Vindel, *Manual*, 2916.

JCB Library copy: Acq: 69–165. Acquired in 1969. Bound in contemporary vellum.

Copies: CtY, RPJCB, InU.

14

TOVAR, JUAN DE, ca. 1546–ca. 1626.

Historia de la benida de los yndios apoblar a Mexico delas partes remotas de Occidente los sucessos y perigrinaciones del camino su gouierno, ydolos y templos dellos ritos y cirimonias y sacrificios, y sacerdotes dellos fiestas, y bayles, y sus meses y calandarios delos tiempos, los reyes que tuuieron hasta el postrero con otras cosas curiosas sacadas delos archiuos y tradicciones antiguas dellos fecha por el padre Juan de Touar de la Compañia de Iesus inuiada al rey n[uest]ro s[eñor] eneste original de mano escrito.

[Between 1582 and 1587]

Collation: 22 cm.: [5], 145, [13] leaves, bound : ill.

Notes: Probably a holograph. Date of MS based on Parry's article; cf. Parry, J. H. "Juan de Tovar and the History of the Indians" (In *Proceedings of the American Philosophical Society*, v. 121, no. 4).

Contents: title leaf (verso blank); leaves [2–4] consist of an interchange of correspondence between Joseph de Acosta and Juan de Tovar concerning the composition of the ms; leaf [5] blank; leaves 1–81 comprise the "Historia"; leaves 82–84 blank; leaves 85–140 contain 29 full-page painted illustrations of Mexican scenes, Indian dances, etc., with a numbered blank leaf inserted before each painting; leaf 141 blank; leaf 142 has the calendar wheel; leaf 143 blank; leaves 144–145 contain "los meses"; leaf [1], blank; leaves [2–12] consist of the Aztec calendar coordinated with Christian one, containing descriptive text and 19 painted illustrations; leaf [13] blank with some ms drawings on recto.

JCB Library copy: Acq: 30289. Acquired in 1947.

Copies: RPJCB.

38

Universidad Nacional Mayor de San Marcos.

Constituciones y ordenancas de la Vniuersidad, y studio general de la Ciudad de los Reyes del Piru.

Impresso en la Ciudad de los Reyes [Lima] : Con licencia del señor visorey don Luis de Velasco, por Antonio Ricardo, natural de Turin., MDCII. [1602]

Collation: 29 cm. (fol.): †8 A–K6 L4 (E1 missigned D1). [8], 46, [18] leaves : ill.

Notes: Title vignette: emblem of the Universidad Nacional Mayor de San Marcos. Errata statement on leaf [6] verso, 1st count. Includes index.

References: JCB Lib. cat., pre-1675, II:18; Sabin, 41091; Medina, *Lima*, 14; Palau y Dulcet (2nd ed.) 59878.

JCB Library copy: Acq: 03767. Acquired in 1868. Bound, in contemporary vellum, with: Constituciones añadidas / Universidad Nacional Mayor de San Marcos. Madrid, 1624. This copy has duplicates of leaves [2] and [5], 1st count.

Copies: NᶜD, RPJCB.

35

VALDIVIA, LUIS DE, 1561–1642.

Doctrina christiana y cathecismo en la lengua allentiac, que corre en la ciudad de S. Iuan de la Frontera, con vn Confessonario [*sic*], Arte, y Bocabulario breues. / Compuesto por el padre Luys de Valdivia de la Compañia de Iesus, de la prouincia del Peru.

En Lima : Por Francisco del Canto., Año. M.DC.VII. [1607]

Collation: 14 cm. (8vo): A–B8 C4 π8 ²A8 D8 E² (²A7ᵛ, ²A8, E2ᵛ blank). 20, 14, [12] leaves.

Notes: Title vignette: Jesuit trigram. "Confessionario breve" (leaves 14–20), "Arte y gramatica" (leaves

1–14, second count, and [1–2]), and "Vocabulario breve" (leaves [3–12]) each has special title page with the same imprint and Jesuit trigram as the main title page.

References: Sabin, 98328; Medina, *Lima*, 39; Viñaza, *Bib. española de lenguas indígenas de Amér.*, 121; Backer-Sommervogel, VIII:378; Palau y Dulcet (2nd ed.) 347831.

JCB Library copy: Acq: 28597. Acquired in 1940. Bound in contemporary vellum with Jesuit trigram stamped in gold on front and back covers.

Copies: MH, RPJCB.

58

VEGA, GARCILASO DE LA, 1539–1616.

La Florida Del Ynca. Historia Del Adelantado Hernando de Soto, Gouernador y capitan general del Reyno de la Florida, y de otros heroicos caualleros Españoles è Indios; escrita por el Ynca Garcilasso de la Vega, capitan de su Magestad, natural de la gran ciudad del Cozco, cabeça de los Reynos y prouincias del Peru. . . .

Con licencía de la santa Inquisicion. En Lisbona. Impresso per Pedro Crasbeeck. Año 1605. Con priuilegio Real.

Collation: 19.5 cm. (4to): 9 p.l., 351 numb. l., [12] p.

Notes: Privilege (p.l. 2ᵛ) dated 8 Mar. 1605. There is another issue without the date on the t.p.

References: JCB Lib. cat., pre-1675, II:31; Sabin, 98745; Medina, *Bib. hispano-americana*, 502; Palau y Dulcet (2nd ed.) 354790; Church, *Discovery*, 329.

JCB Library copy: Acq: 0290. Acquired in 1846. Bound in contemporary vellum. In this copy there is a blank leaf following the 9th prelim. leaf and a blank leaf at the end.

Copies: RPJCB, MB, MBAt, MH, MWA, MHi, NHi, ViU, TˣU, PU, PBL, NIC, CCC, NᶜU, DC, NᶜD, OCU, PHi, CU, NN, MiU-C, PPL, CtY, DLC, CU-A, InU, MnU, TU, KyU, WA, CaBViPA.

42

VEGA, GARCILASO DE LA, 1539–1616.

Primera Parte De Los Commentarios Reales, Qve Tratan Del Origen De Los Yncas, Reyes Que Fveron Del Perv, De Sv Idolatria, Leyes, Y gouierno en paz y en guerra: de sus vidas y conquistas, y de todo lo que sue aquel Imperio y su Republica, antes que los Españoles passaran a el. Escritos por el Ynca Garcilasso de la Vega, natural del Cozco, y Capitan de su Magestad. . . .

Con licençia de la Sancta Inquisicion, Ordinario, y Paço. En Lisboa : En la officina de Pedro Crasbeeck. Año de M.DCIX. [1609]

Collation: 27 cm. (fol.): 10 p.l., 264 numb. l. 1 plate.

Notes: Colophon: En Lisbona. Impresso en casa de Pedro Crasbeeck. Año de M DC VIII. License, dated (2d p.l.v) 2 Sept. 1609. The second part was pub. at Cordoba, 1617, under title: Historia general del Peru. Errata, 10th p.l.

References: JCB Lib. cat., pre-1675, II:61; Sabin, 98757; Medina, *Bib. hispano-americana*, 549; Palau y Dulcet (2nd ed.) 354788.

JCB Library copy: Acq: 01816. Acquired in 1851.

Copies: MiU, WaU, ViU, CtY, IEN, MB, MH, NNH, MWiW-C, DLC, InU, RPJCB, NN, MBAt, CSmH, NHi, MiU-C, NNC, MnU, PPRF.

63

VENEZUELA.

[Constitución (1811)]

Constitucion federal, para los estados de Venezuela, / hecha por los representantes de Margarita, de Mérida, de Cumaná, de Barínas, de Barcelona, de Truxillo, y de Carácas, reunidos en Congreso general.

Caracas. : En la imprenta de Juan Baillio, impresor del Supremo congréso de los Estados-Unidos de Venezuela., Año segundo de la independencia 1812.

Collation: 22 cm. (4to): [A]–E4. 40 p.

Notes: Dated at end: December 23, 1811. There is another issue with an errata statement at the end. Title vignette.

References: Grases, *Historia de la imprenta en Venezuela*, 96; cf. p. 134.

JCB Library copy: Acq: 79–110. Acquired in 1979.

Copies: RPJCB.

FRONTISPIECE

XEREZ, FRANCISCO DE, b. 1500.

[Verdadera relación de la conquista del Perú]

Uerdadera relacion de la conquista del Peru y prouincia del Cuzco llamada la Nueua Castilla : conquistada por el magnifico y efforçado cauallero Francisco Piçarro . . . / embiada a su magestad por Francisco de Xerez . . .

Fue vista y examinada esta obra por mandado de los señores inquisidores del arçobispado de Seuilla : [y] impressa en casa de Bartholome Perez, en el mes de julio. Año del parto virginal mil [y] quinientos y treynta y quatro. [1534]

Collation: 28 cm. (fol.): π1 A2 B–C8. [38] p.

Notes: There are two known issues of this work, the second of which, contains numerous typographical errors on leaf B. Cf. Alden. Illustrated title page. "La relacio[n] del viage que hizo el señor capitan Herna[n]do Piçarro . . ." signed: Miguel Estete (p. [26–33]).

References: JCB Lib. cat., pre-1675, I:116; Alden, *European Americana*, 534/35.

JCB Library copy: Acq: 7649. Acquired in 1911. The issue with typographical errors on leaf B; closely trimmed with slight loss of text.

Copies: NN, CSmH, RPJCB.

54

YAPUGUAY, NICOLAS.

Sermones y exemplos en lengua guarani / por Nicolas Yapuguay ; con direction de un religioso dela Compañia de Iesus.

En el pueblo de S. Francisco Xavier [Paraguay] : [s.n.], Año de MDCCXXVII. [1727]

Collation: 22 cm. (4to): π2 A–I4 Y4 K–V4 X2 (–X2) A–H4 V4 I–K4 L2 (–L2) M4 +[23] unsigned leaves (leaf 23 blank). [4], 64, 63–137, 137–164, 164–165, [1], 98, [46] p.

Sometimes attributed to Paolo Restivo who may have been the editor of this work; cf. *Historia y bib. de las primeras imprentas rioplatenses*, v.1, p. 409—410. Numerous errors in pagination.

References: *Historia y bib. de las primeras imprentas rioplatenses*, 21; Backer-Sommervogel, VI:1677; Viñaza, *Bib. española de lenguas indígenas de Amér.*, 287; Palau y Dulcet (2nd ed.) 262769.

JCB Library copy: Acq: 71–324. Acquired in 1971. Bound in contemporary vellum. This copy lacks p. [1–44], at end (cf. *Historia y bib. de las primeras imprentas rioplatenses*, v.1, p. 402), but does have the blank leaf (p. [45–46]) at end. This copy also has duplicates of p. 81–98, 2nd count, and an extra blank leaf inserted between p. 8 and 9, 2nd count.

Copies: RPJCB.

I

ZUMÁRRAGA, JUAN DE, 1468–1548.

Dotrina breue muy p[ro]uechosa delas cosas q[ue] p[er]tenecen ala fe catholica y a n[uest]ra cristiandad en estilo llano p[ar]a comu[n] intelige[n]cia. /

Co[m]puesta por el reuere[n]dissimo S do[n] fray Jua[n] Çumarraga primer ob[is]po d[e] Mexico. Del Co[n]sejo d[e] Su Magestad.

Imp[re]ssa e[n] la misma ciudad d[e] Mexico : Por su ma[n]dado y a su costa., Año d[e] M.dxliij [i.e. 1544].

Collation: 21 cm. (4to): a–k⁸ l⁴ (l4ᵛ blank). [168] p.

Notes: Title within illustrated border. Colophon reads: Imp[re]miose en [e]sta gra[n] ciudad d[e] Tenuchtila[n] Mexico . . . en casa de Jua[n] Cro[m]-berger por ma[n]dado d[e]l mismo señor ob[is]po do[n] fray Jua[n] Çumarraga y a su costa. Acabo se de imprimir a.xiiij. dias del mes de Junio: del año de .M.d. quare[n]ta y q[ua]tro años. There are several known variants of this work which are described in García Icazbalceta.

References: JCB Lib. cat., pre-1675, 1:139; Medina, *México*, 8; Sabin, 106398; García Icazbalceta, *Bib. mexicana* (1954 ed.), 4; Harrisse, *Americana*, 249.

JCB Library copy: Acq: 07504a. Acquired in 1896. Line 5 of leaf d1 recto reads: ros y guarde la regla de la sctã escriptura que dize. Noliet crede-; line 26 of the same leaf ends: Abrenu[n]cias sathane: y el respo[n]dio; line 25 of leaf d2 recto begins: mie[n]to es d'los vanos desseadores; line 19 of leaf d2 verso begins: venir sino por inspiracio[n]; and line 22 of the same leaf begins: scie[n]tes. Allende. This copy is bound with a facsimile of the last 2 leaves of: [Manual de adultos], Mexico, 1540.

Copies: DLC, NNH, PPRF, MiU-C, CSmH, MH, NN, RPJCB.